The Riverman's Guide to the Kings River

Kayaking, Canoeing, and Fishing, the Kings River in Arkansas

Doug "Riverman" Allen

The Riverman's Guide to Kings River

by Doug Allen

Published by Doug Allen

Fayetteville, Arkansas

www.KingsRiverArkansas.com

© 2021 Doug Allen

All rights reserved. No portion of this book may be reproduced in any form without permission from the publisher, except as permitted by U.S. copyright law. For permissions contact:

KingsRiverArkansas@gmail.com

ISBN: 978-1-7376074-0-3

Cover Photo by Harrison Sutcliffe

The beautiful cover photo of what the locals call Razor Bluff is courtesy of Harrison Sutcliffe and was taken about 6 miles below the Marble public access.

Contents

Acknowledgements 6

Introduction/ The Plan of this Book 9

  I.   Geographical Overview 11

      Course 11

      Watershed 13

  III. History 15

      Early History 15

      Early Conservation 16

      Current Conservation Problems 18

      Ownership and Public Use 21

  IV. Recreation 25

      Regulations 26

         Water Level 26

         River Trip Checklist 29

      Kings River Preserve 30

         Outfitters and Guides 31

         Floating Options 33

            (Legend J. D. Fletcher) 44

         Floating Equipment 47

      Fishing 49

         Bait 50

            (Legend Pat Hanby) 60

	Fishing Gear 62
	Fishing Ethics 64
V.	Wildlife 65
	Fish of the Kings River 65
	Mammals 76
	Birds 76
	Snakes 78
	(Legend Bud Stoppel 79
VI.	About the Author 85
	Background 85
	Riverman Memories 87

Bridges of the Kings River 102

Information Resources 104

Acknowledgements:

"Fishing brings people together. You catch more fish telling stories that night than you do fishing that day. "
~ Doug Allen, April 2019

    This book would not have been possible if it wasn't for the influence and teaching from my dad, Steve Allen, the original Riverman; my mom, Wanda Allen, the greatest barehanded crawdad catcher of all time; my uncle and marine biologist Dr. Kenneth O. Allen; and my river family Pauline, Rachel, Aisling and Charlie. Your patience, love, encouragement and knowledge are strongly reflected in this book. Thank you for understanding how passionate I am about the amazing and beautiful Kings River that I call home. Very few things are ever accomplished alone by anyone. A special thank you to many legends, friends, fishing buddies, and stewards of the Kings River that have inspired, influenced, or encouraged me to write this book for you and future Kings River lovers to enjoy.

    Ernie Killman

    Joe Head

    Donovan Meyer

    Jed Bullock

    Bud Stoppel

    J.D. Fletcher

    Jeff Fletcher

    Pat Hanby

    Carol Wright

    Lin Welford

Angela Belford

Brooks Swink

Bill & Gail DeWeese

Harrison Sutcliffe

Joe Swafford

Phil Dixon

Stan Allen

Jackson Butt

A special 'thank you' to Brooks Swink for his amazing river maps that he spent countless hours and tedious work creating, and to the Kings River Watershed Partnership for great information on Land Use and Gravel Mining.

We all live downstream....

Left to right: Danny Birchfield, Gary Morrell,
Curtis Trammel, Gerald Morrell

I. INTRODUCTION AND PLAN OF THIS BOOK

"Many men go fishing all of their lives without knowing that it is not the fish they are after."
~ Henry David Thoreau

For the fisherman, floaters, river lovers, and eager greenhorns of all ages and skills-the Kings River is calling you. It's calling you to learn, experience, and enjoy every meandering bend of its peaceful shore from the headwaters in the Boston Mountains to its final destination in the Table Rock Lake. A river traversing 90 miles northward through Madison and Carroll counties in Northwest Arkansas, needs an extensive guide with detailed descriptions to teach and entertain while providing history and geological facts about the terrain.

Thorough guide maps help you plan your trip to the river while the Riverman Tips are essential for understanding the regulations, reading the river levels, choosing the right floating vessel, selecting the right fishing gear, and picking the right bait. The Smallmouth Bass reigns supreme over the Kings River, sharing the habitat with over 215 species of fish. While this book is comprehensive in love and lore, time and space will dictate focusing on the most popular sought-after game fish that populate this beloved Ozark stream.

With five decades of familiarity with this free-flowing waterway, I'll share the treasure map of public access points, outfitters you can trust, and infamous legends of the Kings. Perhaps the lack of publications comes from a desire to keep this lesser-known treasure only accessible to the locals; however, I feel obligated to pass on my river knowledge so we can all appreciate and protect the beauty of one of Arkansas' greatest mountain streams. Future generations of fishermen and paddlers depend on us to preserve both the beauty and tranquility as well as the stories and history of this royal stream.

Please join the contribution to this history and body of knowledge by sharing your photos, legends, or other interesting facts via our Kings River Facebook page or our website www.KingsRiverArkansas.com.

Let's remember, we all live downstream.

"If I fished only to capture fish, my fishing trips would have ended long ago."
~ Zane Grey

II. GEOGRAPHICAL OVERVIEW

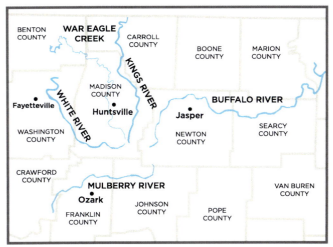

© 2021 Doug "Riverman" Allen

COURSE

Arkansas is a freshwater floater and fisherman's paradise. One of the state's most underrated rivers and "dream stream" of the Ozarks is the Kings River. With the majority of its clear, cool water flowing through Madison and Carroll counties, located in Northwest Arkansas, it is often overshadowed by the popularity of our national river, the beautiful and majestic Buffalo River. The Kings River and the Buffalo River, high up in the Boston Mountains, share their origins just a few miles from each other. Within a ten-mile radius, the White River, War Eagle Creek, and Little Mulberry Creek, also form in these oak tree covered mountains of the Ozark National Forest. Other notable streams that have their headwaters located in the Boston Mountains are the Illinois River, the Mulberry River, Lee Creek, Frog Bayou, Big Piney Creek, Illinois Bayou, and the Little Red River. The Kings River is born at an elevation of more than 2,000 feet on the north ridge of the Boston Mountains located near a small community called Boston. Topographical relief is characterized by beautiful rolling hills, bluffs, oak forests, and some prairie. Physical attributes of this upland region are clear, cold, high gradient, spring fed streams with gravel bottoms and frequent limestone outcroppings. This protected tributary of the White River is undammed and bordered by rural and forested land. It is a popular river for camping, kayaking, canoeing, and sport fishing. Some of the best Smallmouth Bass fishing in Arkansas can be found on the Kings River.

The Kings River rivals the Buffalo and other popular Arkansas streams with tall bluffs, unpolluted clear water, numerous large gravel bars, along with excellent fishing and wildlife habitats. High up in the Boston Mountains, near the headwaters, the Kings River generally flows north. It is full of energy, cutting through sandstone, shale, and limestone, making its way through a beautiful public access area called Kings River Falls. This idyllic area in Madison County has  an access trail nicely maintained by the Arkansas National Heritage Commission with the help of many Arkansas Master Naturalist volunteers. The Heritage Commission's primary goal is to conserve Arkansas's natural landscape for future generations to enjoy and the Heritage Commission does a fantastic job with the beautiful Kings River Falls. A few miles down river near Kingston, the Kings River slows and meanders the rest of the 90 miles through two counties of Arkansas

(Madison and Carroll), until it empties into the beautiful Table Rock Lake in Missouri. The underlying geology along its twisting path includes chert, limestone and dolomite from the Pennsylvania and Mississippi age. Due to the limestone rock formed along the river millions of years ago, karst features can be found, such as water-bearing fractures, caves, and sinkholes. The Missouri portion of the river and its confluence with the White River is flooded and dammed to form Table Rock Lake.

The Kings River is often referred to as two different sections. The upper Kings above the Hwy 62 Bridge between Eureka Springs and Berryville and the lower Kings below the same highway bridge. The largest tributaries to the Kings River are the Osage and Dry Fork creeks, with Osage Creek being the largest. The confluence of Osage Creek and the Kings River

Harrison Sutcliffe Photography

is located at the J.D. Fletcher Public Access by the Hwy 62 Bridge near Berryville, which is aptly named after fishing legend and guide J.D. Fletcher. Other notable creeks are Rockhouse Creek, Felkins Creek, Maxwell Creek, Dry Fork Creek, and Keels Creek.

KINGS RIVER WATERSHED

Although the Kings River is beautiful and magnificent, it is fragile and at the mercy of landowners, cities, and the people using it for recreation. The Kings River Watershed, which totals 591 square miles, is still mostly rural but has seen a significant increase in population over the last decade. The main area of growth comes from two cities, Berryville and Eureka Springs, which reside in the watershed. With the added pressure that comes with population increase, it's important we pay attention, appreciate, and preserve, this extraordinary water source for all future generations to enjoy. Great smallmouth streams are in limited supply and the number becomes even smaller with the encroachment of progress. Other major smallmouth streams of note in Arkansas include; Crooked Creek, Buffalo River, Caddo River, Mulberry River, Ouachita River, Illinois River, and the Upper White River.

Most of the waters within the Kings River watershed are in excellent shape and are monitored by the Arkansas Department of Environmental Equality. For a current list of locally impaired waterways within the Kings River Watershed, and a detailed map, visit the KRWP website at www.KingsRiverWatershed.org.

Harrison Sutcliffe Photography

III. HISTORY

EARLY HISTORY

In the early historic times of Arkansas, the Kings River was a hunting territory of the Osage Native Americans. The largest tributary Osage Creek, which joins the Kings River near the Hwy 62 Bridge near Berryville, was aptly named after the Osage Native Americans that lived in this fertile area of the Ozark Mountains. Occasionally, arrowheads can be found along the river banks that might have belonged to an Osage Native American traveling from Missouri to the hunting grounds in Arkansas or perhaps a Cherokee Native American that made the Ozarks their home. Early European settlers encountered many Osage and Cherokee tribe members in Arkansas and established trade by bartering goods and supplies for furs and skins taken by the Native Americans. Their territory that included the Kings River was fertile with these valuable items Europeans eagerly sought to ship down the Mississippi River all the way to New Orleans in Louisiana.

One of the first Europeans to reach the Kings River was an explorer named Henry King. Not much was written or documented, except he was originally from Lauderdale County in Alabama. In the fall of 1827, he made his way to Northwest Arkansas and the Boston Mountains on a prospecting expedition with two other men, Thomas Cunningham and John J. Coulter. Accounts of his death and resting location are unknown but he is said to be buried on the banks of the Kings River that bears his

Harrison Sutcliffe Photography

name. There were also other families from Alabama who settled in the area. Names such as Madison County, Kingston, and Alabam, testify to early settlers migrating from that state. From the early 1800's to the early 20th century, these early European settlers dramatically altered forests through land clearing and timber harvesting which resulted in a decline of forested land.

The Native Americans also used fire to control understory brush to make the game easier to hunt. Subsistence farming was the main source of employment for many years until poultry farming was introduced around 1940. Fertile land near the river was cleared to build poultry houses for chickens and pastures were made to raise cattle.

EARLY CONSERVATION

"As fishermen, we are the primary users of the habitat so we must also be the primary stewards of the habitat. We all live downstream...."

Destruction of warm water fishing habitat limited many Arkansas streams for smallmouth fishing. President Franklin Roosevelt signed the Flood Control Act of June 28, 1938, which was written to control flooding as well as providing hydroelectricity on the Mississippi River and its tributaries. The White River System in Arkansas was a target of this act as a result of some major flooding during this time.

Fishing didn't figure into the plans of building the dams of many Ozark Rivers. As dams were built and rivers became colder, trout were introduced and soon took the place of Smallmouth Bass (green trout) who couldn't thrive in such a cold environment. The White River was once known as the best smallmouth stream in the country before the dams were constructed. Many lakes were formed by damming up the White River and its tributaries. Beaver Lake, Table Rock Lake, Bull Shoals Lake, Norfork Lake and Greers Ferry Lake, were all man-made lakes built for a state that had very few natural lakes of its own. The Kings River was targeted during the same era as the damming of the White River System and was almost dammed near Grandview (Carroll County) in 1951 as another flood control effort by the U.S. Army Corps of Engineers. The dam was never constructed making the Kings River one of the few undammed protected rivers in the Ozark Mountains.

The Kings River was the first stream in Arkansas to receive legislative recognition and protection. It is designated as an Extraordinary Resource Waterway by the State of Arkansas. These waterways are characterized by scenic beauty, aesthetics, scientific values, broad scope recreation potential, and intangible social values. There can be no physical alterations of instream habitat. Bacteria concentrations must meet swimmable standards year-round. All point pipe discharges must meet advanced treatment technology and the highest level of pollution prevention is required for new road and bridge construction, major pipeline construction, and solid waste disposal sites. Only 16% of Arkansas' total stream miles have been designated as an Extraordinary Resource Waterbody. How fortunate it is to have the Kings River be one of them!

CURRENT CONSERVATION PROBLEMS

"That plastic bottle you threw away? It might end up in YOUR creek. Probably make its way to MY river. Good chance of it landing in YOUR lake. Might end up in OUR Ocean. Make an extra effort to recycle. We all live downstream." ~That's my Dougism for today.

GRAVEL MINING

Unfortunately, gravel is found in abundance along the Kings River because of destabilization and erosion caused by many years of land use changes both upstream and downstream. Commercial gravel mining is illegal on the Kings River but is still legal on its tributaries. A permit from the Arkansas Department of Environmental Quality must be obtained for all commercial gravel mining operations. Gravel should never be removed from the channel itself even if the stream is not currently flowing. Commercial gravel operations are not allowed to operate on the Kings River because of its designation as an Extraordinary Resource Waterway. Contact the ADEQ Mining Division to file a complaint about illegal mining activities.

Contrary to popular belief, gravel mining will not reduce the total amount of gravel in the stream channel. In fact, gravel mining can cause an increase in the total gravel load If gravel is taken out of a stream channel, the river changes in order to regain the natural slope of its streambed. This means it will take gravel from an upstream site, usually from a stream bank, in order to level off the hole that has been created by gravel mining. Gravel mining can directly cause upstream and downstream stream bank erosion. Effects can reach as far as 7 miles.

The effects of gravel mining may not be immediately obvious because only heavy rain events (over two inches) result in large-scale gravel movement. Bank erosion and channel instability upstream and downstream of the mining site become obvious during these larger flooding events. During some years, these storm events are infrequent on the Kings, so there may be a lag of several years before the effects of in-stream gravel mining are evident.

Gravel mining can also negatively impact aquatic species through increases in silt and turbidity. A study of gravel mining on the Kings River showed a 50% reduction in Smallmouth Bass populations downstream of gravel mines.

STREAM BANK EROSION

Stream bank erosion is a major issue for many landowners living along the Kings River and its tributaries. Soil loss from eroding stream banks is the number one threat to water quality on the Kings River. The river can erode acres and acres of usable land every time it is swollen by rain. It is not uncommon for landowners to lose as much as 20 feet of prime pasture in a year with numerous floods. Although some erosion does occur naturally along every waterway, erosion problems along the Kings have been exasperated in recent years. Erosion can occur gradually over time with bank movement hardly noticeable. It can also occur in short, dramatic bursts as a result of extremely high flows or the loss of a streamside tree. Much of the stream bank erosion that occurs on the

Kings River could be easily prevented through protection of the streamside vegetation known as the riparian buffer zone. A riparian buffer zone is a vegetated area that exists next to a waterway. Riparian zones are periodically flooded so they usually consist of vegetation types tolerant to water saturation. These areas act as a buffer between upland activities, such as agriculture or development, and the stream corridor. Riparian buffers along the Kings River can be found in all shapes and sizes because of both natural factors and landowner priorities. Whatever use a property has, there is a type of riparian buffer that could and should be implemented to protect the landowner's investment. The most important action could be taking no action at all by leaving the vegetation undisturbed which will reduce soil erosion and water pollution.

Bank stabilization methods can be structural, vegetative, or a combination of both. Vegetative stabilization methods are those that use plants or plant cuttings to stabilize the bank. When the angle of the eroded stream bank is too steep or the rate of erosion is extremely rapid, structural controls might be necessary to stop loss of property. Structural stabilization methods are those that rely on riprap and/or large boulders to anchor the bottom of the bank, redirect erosive flows away from a portion of the bank, or armor the entire bank with a protective shield. These methods should only be considered when vegetative approaches are not possible due to extreme erosion and stream bank instability.

The Nature Conservancy has been a valuable resource to help manage the big job of stream bank restoration projects along the Kings River. Two recently completed projects include Mason Bend, and the The Oxbow and Rockhouse Creek. All of these projects are between the Rockhouse public access and Kings River Outfitters. These restoration projects prevent a stunning 9,000 tons of sediment, 1,900 pounds of phosphorus, and 4,100 excess pounds of nitrogen, from entering the Kings river annually.

OWNERSHIP AND PUBLIC USE

Ownership of streambeds and usage rights involving streamside properties is an extremely complicated issue. It is beyond the scope of this book to detail the legal definitions and court rulings in this matter.

Please seek a lawyer's opinion for specific answers to ownership issues.

THE ARKANSAS NAVIGABLE RIVERS LIST

In Arkansas, landowners can own the bed of a stream unless it has been determined the stream is navigable. The river bed up to the high water mark of a navigable stream actually belongs to the state of Arkansas to hold in trust for the public. The high water mark is where most of the vegetation stops, and where water movement is so common in ordinary years it makes a distinctive line between the streambed and the stream banks. This line can be very difficult to determine if extensive stream bank erosion exists. The high water mark is NOT the highest point a river reaches during flood stage. When most people think of navigability, they think of giant barges moving up the river. In 1980, the Arkansas Supreme Court expanded the definition of navigability to include recreational use with its decision the Mulberry River is indeed navigable (State v. McIlroy 268 Ark.277). Under the decision, rivers used for recreational use, for even part of the year during normal flow, could be considered navigable by the State.

The river bed of a non-navigable stream is presumed to belong to the adjacent property owner (called a riparian owner). This boundary line could change with the movement of the stream adding or taking away from the total property of a streamside landowner. If a non-navigable stream is determined to be navigable, ownership of the stream bed is transferred to the state of Arkansas. A large portion of the Kings River is used by boaters throughout the year. Does this mean it is considered navigable and the state of Arkansas owns the streambed? The legal determination does not happen automatically just because the boaters use the river; it can only be made by the circuit courts in accordance with Arkansas State Legislature Acts 1854-5, which deems the Kings River in Madison County from the mouth of the Dry Fork to the county line of Carroll County, as navigable.

Navigability and public use of the Kings River falls into a gray area because the private versus public rights have not been challenged in court. That is not a bad thing....it just means we are all getting along.

PUBLIC USE OF WATERWAYS

The public has a clear legal right to use navigable waterways in Arkansas up to the high water mark. However, the public cannot cross private land to gain access to the navigable waterway.

Public access on non-navigable waterways has also been supported through Arkansas property law. If a thoroughfare has been used continuously for seven years with the knowledge but not permission of the owner, the public's legal right to access could be protected through a prescription easement. Prescriptive easements traditionally extend only to the thoroughfare itself, and not to surrounding lands. Generally the judge granting the prescriptive easement defines the terms of use, i.e. how and where specifically the public could use the stream corridor. Crooked Creek in Marion County is a local example of a stream with a prescriptive easement placed on it as a result of a court case.

The Kings River is currently used regularly for many recreational activities although neither a prescriptive easement nor navigability standard have legally been placed on it. The

Arkansas Game & Fish Commission owns five access points to the Kings River, Marble, Rockhouse, Hwy 62 Bridge, Stoney Point, and Romp Hole.

THE FEDERAL NAVIGABLE RIVERS LIST

As if all of this is not confusing enough, the federal government maintains a separate list of waterways they consider to be navigable. Their list dates all the way back to the original granting of land to each state, at which time the federal government reserved the right to regulate navigable waterways. The federal definition of navigability of the waterway is to support commercial use or interstate commerce, so it is a little different than the Arkansas definition.

The Kings River is not currently on the federal Navigable Waterways List; but it and its tributaries can impact the White River, so it still falls under the Corps' jurisdiction.

Contact the U.S. Army Corps of Engineers or the Arkansas Attorney General's office for more info.

Life is Good on the River
~Doug Allen

IV. RECREATION

Cast after cast into the unknown.
In hopes of not being outsmarted by a fish with a brain no bigger than a pea.
The 10 second thrill of the catch.
The 5 seconds of admiration.
The gentle release and goodbye.
It never lasts as long as you want it to.
And then you do it again...
~Doug Allen

Located high up in the upper Boston Mountains, the headwaters of the Kings River flows through the Kings River Natural Area at a rapid rate with a stream gradient that is considerably steep. The water quality is excellent, cool and clear. The Kings River Natural Area includes about 1,059 acres of pine hardwood in the Ozark National Forest. This part of the river has been classified as a turbulent class III whitewater stream. Canoeing or kayaking is not recommended until you reach the Kingston area near Hwy 74, but there are beautiful hiking opportunities to take its place.

One of the more popular places to hike near the headwater area is Kings River Falls. This trail, which is a little less than one mile long, is well marked and beautifully maintained by the Arkansas Natural Heritage Commission with the help of many Arkansas Master Naturalist volunteers. The short and easy hike travels along the river and past many different varieties of plants, and large sandstone bluffs. The end of the trail will result in some amazing water sculpted rock with a beautiful six foot waterfall as your reward. Kings River Falls is best viewed in the spring or early summer or when there is sufficient rainfall.

REGULATIONS

WATER LEVELS

Understanding how to read the water level of the Kings River is very important when planning your floating, camping or fishing trip. One method that can be used is the Advanced Hydrologic Prediction Service by the National Weather Service. It will give you an observed value and predicted value of the water level according to precipitation in the river basin. This service uses water gauge information on a section of the lower Kings River near the Grandview Bridge. The gauge is positioned and monitored a few miles downstream from the Hwy 62 bridge (J. D. Fletcher Public Access). The gauge info can be found at www.water.weather.gov with a search for the Kings River. These forecasts are updated frequently throughout a 24-hour period and issued year round. These predictions take into account past and future precipitation.

Ideal water levels for recreation can vary according to location or activity. Water level on the upper sections of the

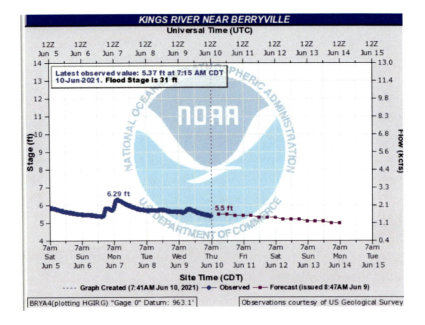

river will not be exactly the same level as the water level on the lower river due to time and distance away from the gauge. For example, 3.5 feet on the water gauge on the lower Kings near Grandview Bridge could mean approximately 3.0 feet on the upper Kings near the Marble public access. It's important to note the predicted rise in water level is not an exact science and should be observed with extreme caution. This river can turn from a gentle meandering stream to a dangerous raging torrent very quickly. Pay attention to the early signs of rising water levels such as a sudden increase in flow, decrease in water clarity, or the appearance of floating debris, such as small limbs or even larger logs that have been displaced by rising and increasing currents.

Harrison Sutcliffe Photography

A good level for canoeing on the Kings River would be from 3.5 to 4 feet deep according to the gauge. This would mean good water clarity and very little dragging during your float trip. With a lighter vessel and better water displacement, kayakers on the lower Kings can utilize the river as little as 2.9 feet if they run the deeper channels. Minimal dragging will occur. No matter what the water level reads, remember that water stops for no one and the force is deceptively strong and dangerous. Always take each turn of the river with respect and caution. When in doubt, get out and scout! There's no harm in walking your canoe, raft, or kayak, around a sketchy area to ensure you live and paddle another day.

"What happens to fish when the river floods?"

During floods or high water periods, fish move to areas where they can hold with the minimum of effort while conserving energy. Usually, this is near the banks, or in cover, like woody debris or large boulders. Even when a river is in flood stage, fish can hold near the bottom if there is enough of a broken substrate to provide them with a "hydraulic cushion," since the friction on the stream bottom is considerably less. There's no question that some fish mortality occurs during floods.

But nature is amazing and they always rebound. The aftermath of bank destabilization and silt deposits from the flood are always major concerns for the health of the river and the fish habitat. Maintaining trees and shrubs along the bank is critical to keeping our waterways as pristine and clear as possible which in turn gives our aquatic species the best chance to survive and thrive.

FLOATING REGULATIONS

Here are some floating regulations for our Kings River waterway that will keep the river beautiful, will keep you safe, and will also keep you from getting an expensive ticket from the game warden.

- Styrofoam and glass are not allowed between the banks.

- A floating beverage holder or "koozie" is required for aluminum cans.

- Flotation devices or life jackets are required per person and anyone under 12 years of age must wear one at all times while floating.

- Coolers and containers must be secured in case of capsize so it doesn't litter our beautiful river.

- A state regulated mesh trash bag must be secured in each canoe or kayak and able to be securely closed.

Each year more and more people frequent the Kings River as the population of Northwest Arkansas grows. It's important we leave as little trace as possible. Take limited food packaging and remove any litter you may find along the way. Pack it in and pack it out. We all live downstream.....

RIVER TRIP CHECKLIST

When planning a trip down the Kings River, there are some essential items to bring with you on any day trip. Packing as lightly as possible is always a good rule of thumb especially when there is little room in a kayak or canoe. A personal floatation device (PFD) is required in all canoes, kayaks and rafts.

- Good river shoes are a must. Don't make the mistake of wearing flip flops and risk either losing them or pulling sharp gravel out of them when wading or dragging your watercraft. An old pair of tennis shoes make the best river shoes!

- A mesh garbage bag is required to make sure no trash is left floating down the river. Secure it to your watercraft. Pick up other trash that you find.

- Bring a Koozie to hold cans or plastic bottles. No glass allowed!

- Always bring plenty of fresh water and never drink untreated river water.

- A small first aid kit to treat scrapes, cuts, stings, and insect bites is a necessity.
- Sun protection that includes sunscreen, hat and sunglasses.
- A dry bag with extra clothes.

"The core of man's spirit comes from new experiences."
~ Jon Krakauer

KINGS RIVER PRESERVE

In 2010, the Nature Conservancy of Arkansas purchased 10.5 miles on both sides of the river to create the Kings River Preserve. It is located in Carroll County near the Rockhouse public access located just upstream from the preserve.

The Nature Conservancy's primary focus in this area is to maintain the health and water quality in the Kings River through stream bank stabilization and reforestation projects to prevent soil erosion. A beautiful deck house and two bungalows overlooking the Kings River valley are located on the preserve and available for rent. Well maintained hiking and biking trails are accessible from the deck house property.

MCILROY MADISON COUNTY WILDLIFE MANAGEMENT AREA

In 1957, the State of Arkansas purchased 14,536 acres of land in Madison County and named it after the McIlroy family that once owned the many acres of this beautiful piece of land. It is located a few miles up river from the Kings River Preserve. This rugged and heavily forested terrain is characterized by many steep mountains and hollows. There are numerous small streams in the area that are tributaries of the Kings River. This management area provides hunting, horseback riding, biking, hiking, and camping opportunities. The

Scenic Overlook is a popular, breathtaking view from a high bluff overlooking this beautiful section of the Kings River.

Did you know...

There is a great story about how the current Hwy 62 Bridge came about in Carroll County. This has neither been confirmed nor denied. Back in the 90's when Mike Huckabee was governor of Arkansas, the dangerously narrow Hwy 62 Bridge over the Kings River was in need of major repair or replacement. The Carroll County judge at the time caught wind of the governor flying into the Berryville airport for a conference in Eureka Springs. He had many failed attempts at convincing the governor and the highway department that a new bridge was needed. The judge conveniently had two very large and wide dump trucks wait at the end of the bridge for the governor. When they saw the governor start across the bridge, they sent the two very large and wide gravel trucks across the dangerously narrow bridge to meet him in the middle. This startled the governor, and soon after he called the county judge to let him know he would get his bridge.

OUTFITTERS AND GUIDE SERVICE

There are three outfitters along what is considered the midpoint of the Kings River. All three of them offer some kind

Doug Allen

of shuttle service and canoe/kayak rental above or below their respective locations on the river. Some offer camping, rentals, and guide service as well. There is also one outfitter located on the upper Kings near the town of Marble.

Map courtesy of Kings River Outfitters

Kings River Outfitters — Located just above the Kings River bridge on Hwy 221. Offering cabin rental, kayak, canoes, and guide service. 479-253-8954
www.KingsRiverOutfitters.com

Riverside Resort — Located next to the Hwy 62 Bridge and J.D. Fletcher public access. Offering cabin rental, canoes, and kayaks. 870-423-3116
www.RiversideResortandCanoes.com

Trigger Gap Outfitter — Located off of Hwy 221 on CR 539. Offering kayaks, canoes, rafts, paddle boards, camping, and guide service. 479-253-5444
www.TriggerGapOutfitters.com

Eddy Out Outfitters — Located at the Marble Access. Offering camping, cabins, canoes, kayaks, and guide service. Shuttle service to the upper Kings River also available. Camp sites, cabin rentals, and cabins available. 918-520-8648

Riverman Guide Service — Offering half day wading or kayak guide service with spincast or fly rod options. 479-790-6491 www.KingsRiverArkansas.com

FLOATING OPTIONS

There are many great floating and fishing options for the beautiful 90 miles of the Kings River depending on the time of year, amount of water flow, and location. The biggest problem for Smallmouth Bass fishermen is choosing which great stretch of water to fish. To help with your floating, fishing, and access decision, five main options are listed with maps. The maps also have elevation lines to help you recognize tall bluffs and turns that could help you decide the scenery and type of water you would like to float or fish. Floaters can start their adventure near Kingston but traditionally the Marble access is the starting point. These are all public accesses and each float has different lengths and approximate times according to time of year and water flow.

Marble to Marshall Ford

Layout, designed, and cussed at by W. Brooks Swink
Printing by Brooks Graphics © 2009

Marble to Marshall Ford

Public Access
Distance — 11.3 Miles
Latitude — 36* 07.30N
Longitude — 93* 30W
Gradient — 5.3ft/mile
Time — 7 hours at minimum floatable water level of 3.5 feet per the USGS gauge.
Recommended early spring to June for good water level.

    This float has an easy public access point near Marble just off Hwy 412. This is traditionally the starting point for many rafting, kayaking, and canoeing visitors. Sections of this river rival the Buffalo River in natural beauty. Large bluffs line this float, along with plenty of rapids with mulTiple twists and turns, to make for an exciting journey. Good stretches of deep pools, large submerged boulders, and other structures make for excellent Smallmouth Bass habitat. It's important to note that you must take portage over a low water bridge. You will have to unload your canoe or kayak and drag them over the left bank of the river. The take out point is at Marshall Ford which is northeast of Alabam on CR 1435. This take out is fairly easy near the bridge but parking is limited to the road.

Marshall Ford to Rockhouse

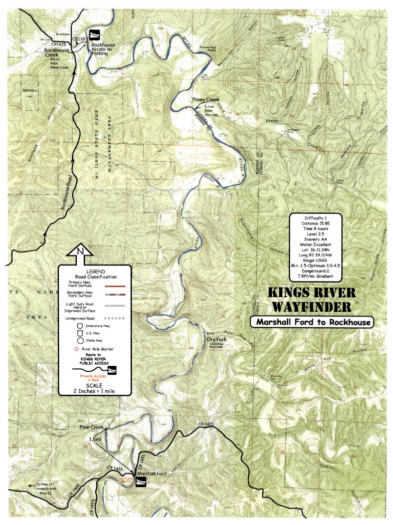

Layout, designed, and cussed at by W. Brooks Swink
Printing by Brooks Graphics © 2009

Marshall Ford to Rockhouse

Public Access
Distance — 15.85 Miles
Latitude — 36° 11.34N
Longitude — 93° 39.104W
Gradient — 7.8ft/mile
Time — 8 hours at minimum floatable water level of 3.5 feet per the USGS gauge.
Recommended early Spring to June for good water level.

There is an easy access point near a small bridge just off of CR 1435 near the town of Alabam, which is a few miles off of Hwy 412. It has paved road access almost all the way to the access point. The parking is limited to just off of a gravel road after the pavement ends. This is a very quiet and attractive float on a gorgeous stretch of river with more beautiful big picturesque bluffs. This long 15-mile float could easily be used for an overnight camp or two on many of its beautiful large gravel bars. Due to the length of the float, you will have the river mostly to yourself. There are many long, deep pools, shallow gravel riffles, eddies, and pools with slow current flowing against boulders and ledges making this prime smallmouth habitat. The take out is very easy at a large gravel bar at the Rockhouse public access (gravel road most of the way) which is just off CR 539 near Rockhouse Creek. Plenty of room for parking.

Rockhouse to Trigger Gap

*Layout, designed, and cussed at by W. Brooks Swink
Printing by Brooks Graphics © 2009*

Rockhouse to Trigger Gap

Public/Private Access
Latitude — 36° 16.19N
Longitude — 93° 39.84W
Gradient — 4.5 ft/mile
Distance — 7.5 Miles
Time — 4 hours at minimum float level of 3.2 feet per the USGS gauge.
Recommended early Spring to June for good water level.

Rockhouse has easy public access with a gravel road most of the way. This access point is just off CR 539 near Rockhouse Creek. There is plenty of room for parking and a very large gravel bar that allows for easy put in. This is a very popular float and a great four-hour day float. You will find more people on this stretch of the river than any other stretch due to easy access and shuttles from outfitters. You will also find very large gravel bars and more of a riparian journey through many twists and turns of the river. Halfway through the float, you meander slowly by land dedicated to the Nature Conservancy. The Nature Conservancy's primary purpose in acquiring the preserve, which spans some 10.5 miles on both sides of the Kings River, is to help maintain the health and water quality of the Kings River. There are remnants of an old, and sometimes impassible, low water bridge toward the end of the float. During high water, it is recommended you portage your canoe or kayak over the left hand side for safety reasons. The take out point is private at Trigger Gap Outfitters or Kings River Outfitters (Mountain Pass) area. You will need to pay a small fee to park your car and use the take out from either one of the outfitters. Stop at their office to make arrangements. They are very knowledgeable of the area and great stewards of the Kings River. They can also provide a complete shuttle service and canoe/kayak rental with different lengths of river options.

Trigger Gap to Hwy 62
(J.D. Fletcher Public Access)

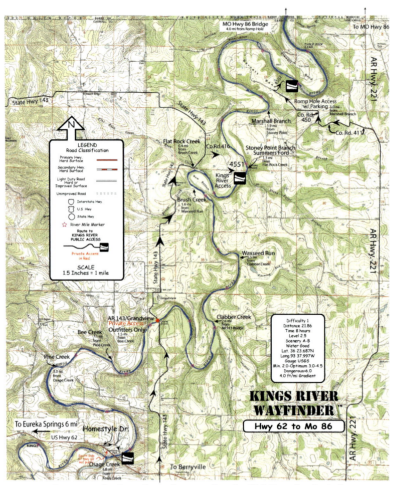

*Layout, designed, and cussed at by W. Brooks Swink
Printing by Brooks Graphics © 2009*

Trigger Gap to Hwy 62 (J.D. Fletcher Public Access)

Private Access/Public
Latitude — 36° 18.89N
Longitude — 93° 39.81W
Gradient — 4.1 ft/mile
Distance — 12.75 Miles
Time — 7 hours at minimum float level of 3.2 feet per the USGS gauge.
Recommended early Spring to June for good water level.

This is a private/public access point in the Trigger Gap Mountain Pass area called Kings River Outfitters or Trigger Gap Outfitters, located just off paved Hwy 221. You will need to pay a small fee to park your car and use the private access. Stop at their office to make arrangements. They also have a shuttle service with other lengths of float options along with canoe or kayak rental. This stretch is a favorite of the Kings River for rafting, kayaking, and canoeing but it is especially known as a trophy section of the river for Smallmouth Bass. Only one bass may be kept and it must be over 18" in length. This 12-mile trip combines good riparian scenery with good fishing and many large gravel bars. Two creek tributaries enter the river on this stretch. Keels Creek enters on the left at Mile 8, and the Osage Creek, which is the largest tributary to the Kings River, enters on the right near the take out at Hwy 62 bridge. The take out point is called the J.D. Fletcher Public Access point just off of the Hwy 62 Bridge with plenty of parking on a paved lot. Please note the path up and down to the river can be a little steep and difficult with a large gravel bar and up some steep rock steps. This float can also be shortened in half with a take out point at McMullen Farm private access. Both Kings River Outfitters and Trigger Gap Outfitters have permission to use this private access.

42 Doug Allen

Hwy 62 Bridge
(J.D. Fletcher Public Access)
to MO 86 Public Access

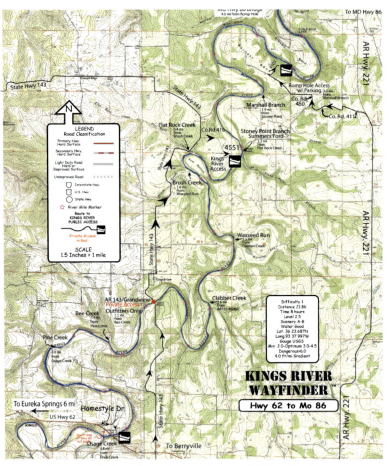

Layout, designed, and cussed at by W. Brooks Swink
Printing by Brooks Graphics © 2009

Hwy 62 Bridge (J.D. Fletcher Public Access) to MO 86 Public Access

Public/Private Access
Latitude — 36° 23.687N
Longitude — 93° 37.997W
Gradient — 4.0 ft/mile
Distance — 21.86 Miles
Time - 14-18 hours at minimum float level of 3.2 feet per the USGS gauge.
Recommended early Spring to August for good water level.

    The J.D. Fletcher Public Access point is just off of the Hwy 62 Bridge. Parking is readily available but please note the path up and down to the river can be a little steep and difficult up a large gravel bar and a few rock steps. The last Kings River trip of what is considered the lower Kings begins here and concludes almost 22 miles near Table Rock Lake. Three-fourths of the way into the trip, floaters will encounter backwaters of Table Rock Lake. This long stretch of river can be broken up into two different floats. The first 12 miles is Hwy 62 to Summers Ford (Stoney Point) Public Access and the next 9 miles is Summers Ford to Hwy 86 Bridge, which is 4 miles down river from another public access called Romp Hole. This stretch of river can be floated later into the summer due to the backup of Table Rock Lake. Plenty of Smallmouth Bass can be found as well as Channel Catfish, Largemouth Bass, and even Walleye, in the deeper pools. White Bass and Walleye can be found seasonally near the lake starting at the Romp Hole, depending on the water temperature and time of year. There are plenty of gravel bars to stop and have lunch. This float is a much slower and easier going stretch of the river. The scenery is mostly riparian with very few bluffs until you get to the lake entrance but it is still a fantastic scenic stretch of beautiful river. To get to Stoney Point, go to Hwy 143 West of Berryville, turn north and go through Grandview. Before you get to Missouri, there will be a brown sign to Stoney Point. A large gravel bar makes it easy to launch a canoe or kayak. The Romp Hole access point is just off of CR 4502 by taking Hwy 221 and turning off of CR 411 to CR 450 and then on to CR 4502. Plenty of parking at the Romp Hole access along with remnants of a boat ramp. The take out at Hwy 86 is private.

Kings River Fishing Legends J.D. Fletcher and son Jeff Fletcher

The first person that comes to mind when thinking about Kings River legends is J.D. Fletcher. You know you're a special person to the Kings River when an access point is named after you. The J.D. Fletcher Public Access at the Hwy 62 Bridge between Eureka Springs and Berryville. Born on November 9, 1930, J.D. grew up on the Arkansas Missouri border in the southwest corner of Ash Township. Laplanders are what they called the folks that overlapped Missouri and Arkansas. As a kid, J.D. cut his teeth along the banks of Sugar Creek learning to fish, and grew up on Greasy Creek near a rural farming community. A creek and community landmark that was important to their way of life. When J.D. was a boy, Greasy Creek cooled milk buried in the gravel, provided habitats for mink trapped along banks, and contributed water for the rural community to boil hogs. The fertile bottom lands of Greasy Creek were used to raise corn, tomatoes, and green beans.

The creek also held a lot of small baitfish and crawdads. There were no bass but many "horny head" minnows and bluegill J.D. liked to catch and sell to the local fisherman.

After high school, J.D. enlisted in the Air Force in 1951 and spent two years serving his country. During his time overseas he longed for home and was quoted as saying; "I'm going back to Missouri and gonna fish the White River." At that time the White River was still undammed and was one of the most widely known and longest stretches of world-class Smallmouth Bass rivers in the country. The White River was eventually dammed to form Table Rock Lake, and J.D.'s attention was turned toward the Kings River.

When J.D. first started fishing he creatively used a hazelnut pole while a lot of people used willow poles. Hazelnut poles were straighter and stronger than the slightly curved willow poles. He used his mom's straight pins, bent them back, and made barbless hooks out of them. With string from a flour sack and a nut from his dad's workshop, J.D. had everything he needed for a fishing pole. Catching fish came early and easy for this Kings River legend.

As a young adult, J.D. moved to Eagle Rock and opened Fletcher's Bait & Tackle near the post office after smartly realizing that Table Rock Lake was being built nearby. He knew that fisherman would come from all over the country and they would need fishing bait and tackle. His parents opened

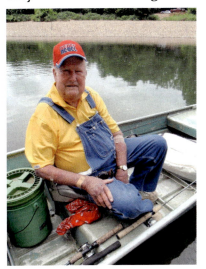

a small restaurant (Fletcher's Dairy Bar) a year later and J.D. ran the bait shop next door selling minnows, crawdads, worms, crickets, and tackle.

In the mid 50's, the Fletchers bought the old Lakeside Motel which had a strip of land that led to the lake. The first boat dock on Table Rock Lake was then constructed. A man named Rube Dick sold his float and guide service to J.D. for $75 that included two heavy wooden jon boats, paddle equipment, and two trailers. Fletcher's Float Service at Fletcher's Devil Dive Resort was born. It was $8 a day for a guided fishing trip with all the J.D. Fletcher ribbing and stories at no extra charge!

J.D. knew everyone, and everyone knew J.D. Fletcher. Pretty soon word got out about the amazing guide trips they were putting together in the Ozarks. TV personalities, athletes, sportscasters, and radio shows hosts, all wanted to spend time with J.D. and his crew. Outdoor Life and Sports Afield all did articles and features about J.D. and the Devils Dive Resort. Famous fishermen Virgil Ward and Jimmy Houston fished with this Kings River legend. With all the press coverage, J.D.'s business took off like a horny head minnow being chased by a Smallmouth Bass. Notable guides that worked for and helped J.D. become successful were Martin King, T.J. King, Bud Stoppel, Charlie Marshall, James Cunningham and Floyd Tate. They were as big as storytellers as J.D., and their customers loved them.

When talking about J.D. Fletcher you might as well be talking about his son Jeff. He was a 'chip off old the block' and one of J.D.'s best homegrown guides that hung around the rest of J.D.'s experienced crew of guides. Stories have been told that Jeff was even weighed on a fish scale at the boat dock when he was born. Of course, the length and weight were exaggerated and a true fisherman was born! Jeff learned from the best and became a guide at a very young age. He went on to graduate with a degree in business administration from the University of Arkansas, fished professionally, and was one of Walmart's first sponsored fishermen. Jeff holds the Arkansas State record striper caught on the White River below Beaver Dam. His striper measured 51 inches in length and 32 inches in girth and was taken with a 12-lb test line. One of the largest stripers ever caught in the United States, his state record fish weighed 64 ½ pounds, shattering the former record of 57. Jeff still guides part time and carries with him years of experience and many memories from fishing and guiding on the Kings River with his dad.

J.D. left a lasting impression with everyone he met. His favorite thing to do was; "Pullin' up on a gravel bar and havin' a good lunch and then a 15 or 20 minute nap. Money can't buy the friendships that I have made since I started the business 43 years ago. People ask me what I like about fishing. I tell them I really don't have to catch fish. I just love to be on the river because of the solitude-no traffic just floatin' down the river. Anyone who's never been on a float trip on the Kings River is missing an experience of a lifetime."

FLOATING EQUIPMENT

There are several vessels that can be used to float the Kings River, depending on what stretch of river you are going to float. Types of vessels used are flat-bottom boats, canoes, kayaks, and motorized boats. Although not as popular anymore and rarely seen, flat bottom boats (Jon Boats) were paddled on all stretches of the Kings River. Flat bottomed boats are either aluminum (typically 12-14 feet) or fiberglass (typically 18-20 feet);

and the earliest Jon boats were made of wood. Many of the early Kings River legends such as Bud Stoppel or J. D. Fletcher could be seen fishing out of an aluminum flat bottom boat.

Canoes are still often seen on the river although molded plastic kayaks have passed them in popularity due to inexpensive cost. In a traditional canoe, the paddler often kneels inside the open cockpit of the vessel and uses a single paddle to propel forward. With two (sometimes three) bench style seats, it's often used in tandem with another person, although it can be paddled solo as well. It takes some skill to paddle a canoe in a straight line. Canoes tend to have more storage space than kayaks and can be much lighter if you have to portage across a gravel bank or obstruction in the river.

In a kayak the paddler is seated and uses a double sided paddle pulling the blade on alternative sides to drive the kayak through the water. Kayaks are often used solo although tandem kayaks can be found. People who like to go alone find that a kayak is easier to paddle and control than the larger canoe. The most common kayak used is a sit-on-top kayak where the paddler sits directly on top in a seat instead of being recessed inside the vessel. Sit-in kayaks are also an option where the paddler is seated inside the vessel. You will find that sit-on-top kayaks are much more stable than a canoe in regards to Tipping over.

Motorized boats can be used on the lower Kings from Romp Hole access to the Hwy 86 Bridge with water being much deeper as it reaches Table Rock Lake and the Missouri state line.

FISHING

"The charm of fishing is that it is the pursuit of what is elusive but attainable, a perpetual series of occasions for hope."
~ John Buchan

FISHING LICENSE REQUIREMENTS

As per the Arkansas Game and Fish Commission, you are required to have a license to catch fish in the state of Arkansas. For the Kings River, a Resident Fisheries Conservation License entitles a resident to fish the waters of the Kings River as well as many other water bodies in the state. Three day, seven day, and one year, Nonresident Fishing License options are also available. Licenses are available at many sporting goods stores or discount chains. You can also obtain a license by phone at 800-364-GAME or online at www.AGFC.com. Prices vary according to residency, age and type of license. Disability and mobility impaired licenses are also available. Please note the Kings River shares a border with Missouri. Therefore, you will need to purchase a border license. This license will allow you to fish the waters of Table Rock Lake. This license is advisable when floating from Romp Hole access to the Hwy 86 Bridge which is part of Table Rock Lake in Missouri.

SMALLMOUTH BASS LIMITS

The Kings River is designated an Ozark Zone Quality Smallmouth Stream, meaning the Smallmouth Bass daily limit is two on the stretch of water described, and each fish must be at least 14 inches long. The section of the river from Trigger Gap to the Hwy 62 Bridge (J.D. Fletcher Public Access) is designated as a trophy section.

The Smallmouth Bass daily limit along the trophy section is one and it must be at least 18 inches long. Catch and release is recommended to help increase the quantity and size of large trophy bass.

Catch and release the right way...

- Pinch the barb on your hook flat so it's easily removed.

- Bring the fish to the boat or shore as quickly as possible to avoid extreme exhaustion.

- Keep the fish in the water and resuscitate it. Handle the fish gently with wet hands. If you must net it, use a release net made of soft knotless fabric and keep the fish under water in the net.

- Have tools and a plan. A simple pair of needle nose pliers will do. Make sure your eyes are covered in case the hook flies free. Locate the hook, then decide how to gently approach it for removal.

- Fish responsibly. Alter your method to minimize hooking mortality. That may mean setting the hook a little sooner to keep aggressive fish from swallowing the hook.

- If we are responsible in our approach today, it will mean more fish in the future for everyone to enjoy.

"Game fish are too valuable to only catch once."
~ Lee Wolff

BAIT

Natural Fishing Bait

The most common natural live bait used to catch most of the game fish of the Kings River include crayfish, minnows, hellgrammites, and worms. These types of natural bait are in abundance and the aquatic baits are also a good indicator of water quality.

Crayfish

In virtually all Smallmouth Bass habitats, and especially the Kings River, crayfish (crawdads) are a substantial protein source in comparison to the effort needed to eat them; they are easier to catch than minnows. When eaten, these protein packed crustaceans will put on weight for a bass. Not only does it contain protein but the exoskeleton contains a wealth of calcium for any predator. The warmer late spring weather and lower water level will have the crayfish active after hibernating underground in colder seasonal temperatures of late fall and winter. Carefully turn over a few larger rocks and you should find a few of these bass favorites. Find a soft shell crawdad that has recently molted and you'll have a bass favorite that they cannot resist. There are several different types of crawdads and hybrids in the Kings River, and each looks and attracts fish differently.

Crayfish are animals called crustaceans. Often called "crawdads." They are arthropods (meaning many segments), and these segments are joined together. Crawdads do not have backbones. They have exoskeletons made of a tough calcium-rich material called chitin. They have ten legs with the two front legs called "chelipeds" that have claws on the end to help defend itself or push food into its mouth. (They can also pinch the fire out of you!) The abdomen is in the crawdad's rear body section, and it is sometimes called the tail. The tail helps it swim backwards during the flight response. These cold-blooded animals hibernate during cold temperatures. Almost every continent in the world has crawdads with the exception of Africa and Antarctica. Luckily there is an abundance of crawdads in Arkansas and especially the Kings River. Turn over any good size rock and chances are you will find a crawdad. A crawdad grows and molts its exoskeleton mulTiple times to become bigger. Many species of fish savor the taste of crawdads over other kinds of natural bait because they emit a strong scent that attracts fish from a considerable distance. This scent is stronger when they have molted. Smallmouth Bass cannot resist a molted soft shell crawdad! It's always a treat to catch a soft shell crawdad with the anticipation of catching a nice smallmouth! Handle with care as they are very fragile and soft after molting their outer shell.

Riverman Tip-

The number one protein source for Smallmouth Bass is crawdads. Crawdads that are about 2-3 inches long are the ideal size to use for live bait fishing. Simply use a #2 shiny gold long shank hook through the inside of the tail, throw upstream and let drift naturally with the current. Look for unusual movement of your line and then set the hook aggressively!

Types of Kings River Crayfish

There are 5 different species of crawdads in the Kings River. The pictures are of the 3 most common species that are easily found in the Kings River. Each species gets a different reaction out of smallmouth due to color, liveliness and size.

Ringed Crayfish

I find these crawdads to be a bit sluggish and bulky when they hit the water. The very Tip of their claws are orange. This type of crawdad can get to a fairly decent size and tend to stay alive longer when used for bait.

Dustin Lynch, Arkansas Natural Heritage Commission

Williams Crayfish

I find these crawdads to be a little more active and aggressive than the ringed crayfish and sometimes you can find one that is bright orange in color that smallmouth can't resist. Their bright color can be seen from long

Dustin Lynch, Arkansas Natural Heritage Commission

distances. This crawdad doesn't stay alive on the hook very long but it usually doesn't matter because there is a hungry smallmouth soon to be caught with it.

Long-pincered Crayfish

This sleek almost alien looking crawdad, greenish in color, can grow to an enormous size. This is probably my favorite crawdad to use for fishing but the hardest to catch because of its speed. Super fast! Once it hits the water, it is super active

trying to get away, causing a commotion that drives the Smallmouth Bass crazy.

Hellgrammite

Often referred to as "smallmouth candy," the Hellgramite is a favorite meal of the Smallmouth Bass. Packed with protein, this fearsome predatory aquatic larval form of the elusive Dobson Fly can be found in the warmer months under small rocks in shallow, slow-moving water. They are very poor swimmers and will not venture far from their hiding place. They can reach up to 3-inches long and have a tough, segmented body with legs on each segment. By their heads, they have prominent, powerful, and sharp pincers, that pack quite a punch!

Dustin Lynch, Arkansas Natural Heritage Commission

Riverman Tip-

Simply hook the Hellgrammite anywhere through the body with a number two or smaller hook. Cast and let drift naturally. Hang on for the ride as it won't be long until you've hooked a fish! All varieties of game fish will strike the Hellgrammite but it is definitely a favorite of the Smallmouth Bass. One Hellgrammite can often be used several times as it has a very tough body and is very hard for the fish to remove from the hook. Use added weight according to water level to get your Hellgrammite down near the bottom.

> *the crawdad*
> *he feels the gravel crunching*
> *and hears the footsteps approaching*
> *and knows the fish are hunting*
> *hungry yet unaware*
> *of the hook and the fate that awaits him.*
> *-Rachel Allen (2018)*

Minnows

Live minnows, or shiners, are abundant and also a Smallmouth Bass favorite. There are many types of small baitfish in the Kings River and they can be caught with minnow traps or seining nets with very minimal effort. Kings River fishing legend, J.D. Fletcher, grew up catching "horny head minnows" in small creeks and tributaries around the Kings River.

Riverman Tip-

To catch a variety of game fish using minnows, simply use a number two size hook and let the minnow swim naturally in the current with little to no weight.

Worms

"Bait fisherman? Good Lord! He's going to show up with a coffee can full of worms. Red can. Hills Brothers. I'll lay a bet on it." This funny but sarcastic quote about bait fishermen is from the book and movie A River Runs Through It. Say what you want about worms. They work. Red worms or nightcrawlers are a natural bait for most game fish and are sure to catch fish most any time of the year.

Riverman Tip-

Simply use just about any size hook, a worm, and a bobber. You can also use a weight with no bobber to get down deep for some channel cats. Worms can entice finicky fish that won't bite anything else. Kings River fishing legend Bud Stoppel used to drive a metal stake in the ground, causing vibrations, and large "night crawler" and other earthworms would rise to the surface.

Artificial Bait

There are thousands of different types of artificial bait that can be used to catch fish. Don't be afraid to experiment with your favorite artificial fish catcher no matter the type of water. In this guide book, I'll focus on the most popular type of artificial baits as well as some I've used with great success on the Kings River.

Soft Plastics

Soft plastics are excellent artificial baits to use on the Kings River. Many methods can be used for tying on a jig but Texas Rigging a variety of soft plastics with different colors can result in a productive day of catching many types of game fish. Some favorite soft plastics may include; tubes, worms, flukes, swimbaits, hellgramites, crawdads, minnows, and lizards. I have found the darker colors work best and the more realistic, the better.

Riverman Tip-

Vary your speed and location of bait placement. Fish hold at different locations according to water level, clarity, and time of day. Don't be afraid to throw into shallow areas you think won't hold fish. You'll be pleasantly surprised.

Jigs

Many types of jigs or lead heads are effective for catching most, if not all, fish of the Kings. They are very potent for fish that are deep or near the bottom. Formed with a single hook and a lead head, the tail offers many different variations for experimenting with buck hair, maribou, pork rind or soft plastics.

Riverman Tip-

Try adding a soft plastic trailer on the end of a jig to enhance the action and visibility. Various sizes and colors can be used according to water depth and clarity. The more tail action, the better result. The locally made Arkie Jig and trailer can entice all game fish of the Kings.

Spinners & Buzzbaits & Topwater Baits

Using a spinner or buzzbait is an exciting way to catch fish. The white beetle spin or different color rooster tails or noisy buzzbaits can get you noticed by a Smallmouth from long distances by the shiny flash or the sound of the blades cutting through the top or just underneath the water surface. Is there anything more exciting than a Smallmouth Bass crushing a topwater buzzbait? The classic Heddon Zara Spook, Strike King Buzzbait, or a Whopper Plopper, top water bait can make many fish explode to the surface.

Crank Baits

Any lure that has a plastic lip causing a bait to dive underwater can be classified as a crankbait. It is a versatile lure of many sizes that can catch fish of all species in all seasons. Rapala Minnows, Arkie Craws, and Crawdad Bombers, with different running depths and colors are all excellent choices for catching Smallmouth Bass.

Flies

Several different types of flies will catch bass and panfish. There are floating bass flies such as poppers or mice. Sinking bass flies such as muddler minnows, and crayfish patterns. Panfish flies such as ants, spiders and worms. There are many variations of all these flies and tying your own fly to catch a fish is one of the most rewarding projects you can do.

Riverman Tip-

The amazing Hada Creek Crawler is one of my favorite crawdad patterns of all time! Bouncing off clean gravel bottoms can result in catching many fish of the Kings River.

"As a child my dad gave me the best advice on catching fish. I did not realize at the time that he was being very serious. He said, "Son you can't catch fish if your bait isn't in the water." "So much truth in that simple statement. And I quote that to a lot of people that I take fishing."
~ Riverman

Technique

I was reflecting upon a few of my recent fishing expeditions and the amazing quantity and variety of fish caught. I realized I'm often asked, "What are you using to catch fish?" My bait selection is usually very small. It's only 2-3 different types of bait as I take the time to learn how to present each one. In the restaurant business, plate presentation can make all the difference in customer selection and satisfaction. The same can be said for presenting an enticing bait to a fish.

There are a lot of anglers that believe "one" magic bait can satisfy their need to catch either the quantity or quality of fish they are after. And that's okay, if it's what they want out of the experience. It's kind of boring if you ask me, so I like to experiment with different types of bait. But not too many at one time on a trip.

I travel light and try to master whatever I'm using. For someone that has caught a lot of river fish in his lifetime through trial and error, this makes it more educational, challenging, and exciting. It satisfies my curiosity and fulfills my desire to learn as much as I can about a whole other world of fish underwater and how those different species react to different stimuli. My belief is you can use just about any type of bait as long as you are mimicking the size and color of what's already in the water. Sometimes the bait doesn't look like anything natural a fish would eat. There's an old saying, "it's not how deep you fish, it's how you wiggle your worm." Without realizing it, there is a mental checklist that runs through my mind before every cast: the position of the throw, the angle, the depth, the substrate, the retrieve, and the aggressiveness of the strike. All of these details and the results will determine how I will fish that day. There are so many different variables when fishing or as I like to say "catching". Compensating for wind, current, and structure obstacles, is always a challenge. Coupling that with fighting the ever-changing and sometimes unpredictable weather with a kayak/canoe gives you quite a challenge. Sunlight, water temperature, and water clarity also play a huge factor. No one said fishing is easy. Catching is way more fun. Fish on!

> *"If you use the wrong bait long enough,*
> *it will soon become the right bait."*
> *~ Riverman*

Kings River Fishing Legend Pat Hanby

One time resident of Berryville and local Kings River legend, Pat Hanby, spent many hours as a kid fishing and floating the Kings River and its largest tributary, Osage Creek, in his flat bottom fiberglass boat. His fishing trips covered mostly the Rockhouse access and the lower Kings downstream toward Table Rock Lake. Pat has fished the Kings River since the 1950's and still does today. He has used various classic artificial baits such as River Runts, Lazy Ike, Lumber Jack Paul Bunyon, 66 Lure, Black Peck, Ding Bat, and the Heddon King Basser. Fishing at night, his favorite lure of choice was the Jitterbug. Most of these classic lures are no longer in production but still remain in Pat's collection of Smallmouth Bass catchers. Big fish were caught by Pat and his brother Phillip using some of those lures in local fishing spots on the Kings River such as the legendary Garret Hole near the Hwy 62 Bridge. The Garret Hole was a deep hole created when Garret Gravel Company dredged gravel out of the river for a couple of decades. In some places in the hole, the depths could reach 20 feet. His biggest trophy Smallmouth Bass of 6-lbs was caught in this very locally known fishing hole and access on the Kings River. It wasn't uncommon for him to snag Red Horse and Suckers from this very same spot using dynamite wire and large treble hooks strung across with large sinkers to weigh it down.

As a young fisherman in the 50's, Pat had a unique way of catching fish. His dad had invented a fishing device using  a small piece of white pine that was in the shape of a paddle. A very stiff monofilament fishing line was attached and wrapped around the small hand held paddle and a hook was attached. A simple toss would cause the line to come off the paddle just like it would come off of a spool from a fishing reel. He could easily toss the line 30 to 40 feet.

Live crawdads were Pat's bait of choice. The bigger the better in order to eliminate the smaller fish of the Kings River. He caught and trapped buckets of crawdads on the river and creeks during the day by turning over large rocks and after dark when they were more active and easier to find. This tough natural bait would easily stay on the hook and entice Smallmouth Bass to bite. After casting out his bait, the paddle could be easily tucked into his shirt to free up his hands to pull and work the crawdad to a bass he would sight fish on the clear Ozark Mountain river. He could position a crawdad upstream from a Smallmouth Bass he located, then watch the hungry bass engulf the crawdad. Always tail first. Working the stiff line and tugging fish would rough up and cut his hands. It was a good day of fishing if he went home with sore and tired hands, along with a stringer of fish. Currently, Pat lives in Springdale and fishes mostly on Beaver Lake but occasionally has a longing for the amazing Smallmouth Bass on the beautiful Kings River where he grew up.

Fishing Gear

Spinning Gear

A favorite of many fishermen of the Kings River throughout the years has simply been an open face spinning reel and a medium action 6-7 foot rod. There are also many other different types and sizes of rod and reels that can be used to catch fish and personal preference and familiarity with your own rig can gather the same results. Six-pound test monofilament line is a great combination with a light spinning rod and reel. When the water is high and there is less visibility, eight-pound test line can be used.

"I had an Old Mitchell Garcia 308 given to me a few years ago by fishing legend Joe Head. My dad had one of these old-timer classic reels that went with a Garcia Rod. It was my dad's favorite rod and reel combo. It has a very distinct "click" when the bail of the reel is opened. Unfortunately, I left it leaning on the truck after we stopped to

fish the Buffalo River. Drove off and left it. My dad was really upset over losing it. Never blamed me. But it was my fault. I've since found a Garcia Rod to match this reel. It hangs in the living room in his honor. I get it down occasionally and catch fish with it and chase a few memories with my dad."
~Riverman

Fly Gear

Fly fishing for game fish on the Kings River can be a lot of fun but quite challenging. The recommended choice of fly rods for trophy Smallmouth Bass would be a heavier weighted fly rod that can throw heavier flies such as crawdad patterns. Sinking versus floating Tip line depends on your preference and presentation but both can be used effectively.

Light fly tackle can be used as well to catch Sunfish, Ozark Bass, Spotted Bass, and even Small and Largemouth Bass, using lighter streamers and poppers.

Catching a trophy Smallmouth Bass on a fly rod will be a fish and a fight you will never forget!

Riverman Tip-

When kayak or canoe fishing down a stretch of river, throw perpendicular to the opposite bank instead of throwing upstream or downstream. (Also make sure your vessel is out of the strike channel.) You will decrease your chance of getting hung-up and spooking the skittish fish. Imagine a hand fan. Working your bait from one side of the fan to the other. You will cover more area using this method and be less likely to miss a fish. Always start your throw at the edge of the bank as there might be a hungry fish waiting. Those fish usually strike fast. Utilizing this simple technique will increase the amount of fish you catch. Tight lines!

FISHING ETHICS

As anglers and stewards of the waters of Arkansas, it's up to us to preserve the river and its habitat to make sure future generations get to enjoy the sport of fishing on the beautiful Kings River for years to come.

- Purchase a fishing license.
- Keep only the fish you can use.
- Practice catch and release.
- Respect property owners rights.
- Know harvest limits and size restrictions.
- Support conservation efforts.

Conversation with my wife, the triathlete, last night.

I call it, *The Understanding-*

Pauline- "You should do triathlons like I do."
Doug- "Sorry but that would cut into my fishing time."

Pauline- "But you would be very good at it."
Doug- "If I have time for triathlons, then I have time to fish."

Pauline- "It would make you more healthy and you would live longer."
Doug- "But don't you understand, fishing already does that."

End of conversation.

V. WILDLIFE

FISH OF THE KINGS RIVER

A river of fish is more complex than you can imagine. Fish are very similar to land animals in terms of being driven by basic instincts of finding food, avoiding being eaten by predators and needing to reproduce. These basic instincts have caused an evolution of body shapes and colors. Most fish spend a large majority of their lives gathering food because they must eat to live. There are several different species of fish that thrive and can be seen in the clear, spring-fed, gravel bottom stream that is the Kings River. There are so many, an entire book could be written about fish alone. This guide book will only focus on the most common fish often seen while floating or caught while fishing along the alluring stretches of the Kings River.

Smallmouth Bass

The King of the Kings! Few fish can outclass the Smallmouth when it comes to the exciting battle between man and fish. Pound per pound Smallmouth Bass are a tough-fighting fish. When catching a Smallmouth Bass, it's not unusual for it to leap and try to shake the hook out of its mouth. If that doesn't work, they dive hard to the bottom for some kind of structure, log or rock. It is a never-quit fish that will fight you all the way to the bank or boat. When measured for pure tenacity and heart, the Smallmouth swims alone. The Smallmouth Bass is a species of freshwater fish in the sunfish family. Sometimes called a brownie, bronze back, smallie, brown bass, or green trout. It is generally brown, appearing sometimes as black or green with red eyes, and dark brown vertical bands, rather than a horizontal band along the side. A distinct feature of "war paint" lines extend from the nose of this warrior fish, on both sides. There are 13–15 soft rays in the dorsal fin. The upper jaw of Smallmouth Bass extends to the middle of the eye which differentiates it from the Largemouth Bass. The Smallmouth's coloration and hue may vary according to environmental variables such as water clarity or prey diet. This clever bass thrives in clear, gravel-bottom runs, and free-flowing pools of rivers. Males are generally smaller than females. The males tend to range around two pounds, while females can range from three to six pounds. Their average sizes can differ, depending on where they are found. Those found in American waters tend to be larger due to the longer summers, which allow them to eat and grow for a longer period of time. Smallmouth Bass have an incredibly wide field of vision (180 degrees). They can see prey or potential danger from many angles and it is a tremendous advantage that they utilize. In clear water, they can see up to 40 feet away. They usually see you before you see them.

> **Did you know...**
>
> Next to vision, one of the smallmouth's most important senses is hearing. When wading or floating down the river, it's key to stay quiet. Smallmouth spook easily to sound. They can hear the crunch of gravel from a good distance or the echo of a paddle hitting the side of your canoe or kayak. Although you may not have ever seen them, Smallmouth Bass have internal ears located on each side of their head.

Their habitat plays a significant role in their color, weight, and shape. River water Smallmouth Bass that live in dark water tend to be rather torpedo-shaped and very dark brown to be more efficient for feeding. Lakeside Smallmouth Bass that live in sandy areas, tend to be a light yellow-brown to adapt to the environment in a defensive state and are more oval-shaped.

Smallmouth Bass have been seen eating tadpoles, fish, aquatic insects, crayfish, and anything they could swallow, they will. They have been seen eating frogs, small mice, and even small birds. Due to the shallowness of the water, which causes water temperatures to fluctuate, Smallmouth Bass usually spawn in early April and can extend into May. Using their tail, Smallmouth Bass sweep their nesting areas clear of debris before the female lays her eggs. They prefer a clean gravel bottom to lay over 2,000 eggs. It is the male that builds and guards the nest. Once the eggs hatch after 5-7 days, the job of the male is over. He has now developed a ferocious appetite and will vigorously attack most any food source in his way. This post spawn period is an excellent and exciting time for Smallmouth fisherman with aggressive strikes on many different types of bait. These fish are fast growers. Freshly hatched Smallmouth feed on zooplankton and other microscopic animals in the water. Once they are an inch or two, they switch their diet to mainly insects or tiny crawfish and some baitfish. Good mineral content, clean silt-free water, plentiful food sources, excellent habitat, and extended growing seasons, can produce very large fish up to 5 pounds. The Kings River has all of these variables to grow trophy-size Smallmouth Bass. Practicing catch and release can help them get there.

Nature designed the Smallmouth Bass as a creature of finicky habits. He cannot tolerate extremely hot or extremely cold water for large periods of time. He cannot tolerate polluted waters and the fact you can find Smallmouth Bass in a stream is an indication of good water quality.

Fall is a great time of year to catch Smallmouth Bass. The beauty and color of the changing foliage of the Ozarks make it much more appealing. The bass have recovered from their spring spawn and have put on some weight throughout the summer. The cooler temperatures have triggered the Smallmouth Bass to start thinking about the upcoming winter and fattening up to get through the starvation period and have enough fat for the spring spawn. Live crawdads will still be available into much of October and will be a good choice of bait. Soft plastics mimicking a crawdad or lizard will work as well. As it gets cooler, the fish will slowly migrate to the deeper holes with structure where they will eventually end up for the winter. You can catch winter Smallmouth in the deeper holes but you have to throw them something big and worthwhile and pretty much get the bait right in front of their noses to have any success. The water will be clear and cold in the winter, and you will rarely see any species of fish swimming freely in the river like you see in the summer. It's a beautiful winter river but a "ghost" river as the fish have hunkered down for a few months. Their heart rate slows and they are conserving energy. You should consider carefully floating the river when there's snow on the ground and in the trees. A beautiful sight to see! Happy Fall fishing and tight lines!

Spotted Bass

Also known as a Kentucky Bass, this Bass is not as dominant as the Smallmouth Bass in terms of numbers but it can get as large and fight almost as hard. It is often mistaken for the Largemouth Bass, and usually found in calm, deep pools, next to tree roots or other large structures. Their diet is very similar to a Smallmouth and can be caught with live minnows, crawfish, lures,

Dustin Lynch, Arkansas Natural Heritage Commission

and flies. It is a very beautiful fish and like the Smallmouth Bass, has a jawline that does not extend past the eye.

The back is dark olive and the sides are yellowish. It has a dark lateral band with rows of black spots beneath. Spotted Bass inhabit areas that are too warm, turbid, and sluggish, for Smallmouth Bass. Like the Smallmouth Bass, the female will fan and clear a nest and lay close to 2,000 eggs while the male will guard the nest. Spotted Bass are likely to be found in groups, which provides the opportunity to catch more than one in a given place. River fishing techniques are pretty much the same as those used for Smallmouth Bass and they will also have a voracious appetite after the spawn.

Riverman Tip-
How to distinguish a Spotted Bass from a Largemouth Bass.

Sometimes it is difficult to tell the difference between the two very similar bass. Spotted Bass have lines of spots along the stomach. Largemouth Bass do not have these spots and generally have a white stomach. The Spotted Bass has a rough patch in the center of the tongue vs the Largemouth Bass that has a smooth tongue. The dorsal fin on a Spotted Bass is clearly connected, with a gentle slope. On a Largemouth Bass, the dorsal fin is separate, or nearly separate. This is probably the most significant distinction between the two species.

Channel Catfish

This elusive, strong, and adaptable fish has a flat wide head while the upper jaw is just past the lower jaw. It has a bluish-gray back, and the belly is white. Its sides are silvery with black or olive spots that lessen with

Dustin Lynch, Arkansas Natural Heritage Commission

age. No scales are present and it has a set of whiskers near its mouth. The Channel Catfish is found in moderate flowing rivers and creeks. They can be found in deep pools with large rocks, logs, and overhanging banks, that protect them during the day. They normally leave their safe spots at night to feed. It is a ferocious fighter when first caught but will fade quickly as it tires. They can be caught on chicken liver, worms, crawdads, live minnows, and jigs. A tough and heat-tolerant fish that can survive temperatures up to 93°F. Channel Catfish spawn from May to June when temperatures reach about 80*F. They lay their eggs in holes or cavities found in an undercut bank, underneath a large rock, or a hollowed, submerged log. The males will build the nest and protect the young fry until they leave the nest.

Spotted Gar

The Spotted Gar has a short snout with one row of teeth and a long cylindrical body. It's brown on the top and lighter on the sides. This intimidating looking fish has a white belly and the entire body and fins are spotted. It has very thick tough scales. The Spotted Gar has a large mouth packed with sharp, pointed teeth. They are generally sluggish fish but are capable of impressive bursts of speed. They usually drift motionlessly near the surface waiting for smaller fish to swim by. When prey approaches, they whip their heads around and snare their victim, often sideways, then turn it to swallow head-first.

One of the reasons they've survived as long as they have is their ability to thrive in even the most inhospitable, murky, low oxygen waters. They have a swim bladder they can fill by gulping air, which they use to supplement their gill-breathing in low-oxygen environments. You can often see them surface to refill with air. The Gar spawn in shallow water in the spring. Usually late April. The adhesive eggs are scattered all over the substrate and sometimes buried in it. Neither the male or female protect the eggs once they are spawned. Different techniques can be used to catch a Gar such as a shiny spinner bait or even small perch. Gar are edible but very bony. It's important to note that Gar eggs are NOT edible and are toxic to humans.

Ozark Bass

The Ozark Bass is a species of freshwater fish in the sunfish family and is often mistaken for a very closely related Rock Bass. It is native ONLY to the White River area of Missouri and Arkansas and nowhere else in the world. It has a very large mouth, red eyes, and scaled cheeks. The sides are irregularly freckled. It can grow up to 10 inches or nearly one pound. The males build nests on gravel substrate and they begin to spawn

Dustin Lynch, Arkansas Natural Heritage Commission

when temperatures reach 62°F. They can be caught on the Kings River using live minnows, crawdads, hellgrammites, and small jigs or crank baits. Ozark Bass are usually found in slow moving pools with large rocks or cover.

Longear Sunfish

This beautiful but small and colorful Sunfish has a moderately small mouth with a wavy line on the cheek and the upper jaw not extending past the middle of the  eye. It can be identified with a long black "ear" flap rimmed red or white. It has a green or blue-green back. It has olive sides splattered with yellow and blue-green spots. The belly is yellow or burnt orange. It has short round pectoral fins. You can find these stunningly beautiful little fish in slower pools with rocky bottoms. They grow to about 9 inches long. Its food consists mainly of aquatic and terrestrial insects as well as live minnows, worms, small crayfish, spinners or poppers. Spawning occurs from May to August when water exceeds 75°F. The males construct circular depression nests close together. The male courts the female by swimming around and above her, displaying his bright red-orange belly. The male may spawn with many different mates. The male will aggressively guard the nest until the fry becomes free-swimming.

Green Sunfish

A real survivor, this fish is able to tolerate low levels of oxygen in the water as well as survive temporary drought conditions. The Green Sunfish has a large mouth compared to  other sunfish. It has an elongated blue-green body. It has a pale green belly with dots in rows on the sides and with black dots on anal and dorsal fins. It is sometimes called a black perch or shade perch. They can grow up to 10 inches in length and reach a pound in weight but most are around 4-8 ounces. They are found mainly next to logs, root balls, or other thick weedy cover near the bank. They have a large mouth and like to eat worms, live minnows, and crawfish. An aggressive and strong fighting fish that can also be caught on artificial baits such as spinners, poppers, and streamers.

Anglers usually catch them by accident while seeking other game fish such as Smallmouth Bass. Green Sunfish begin spawning in the summer. The males create nests in shallow water by clearing depressions in the bottom near a type of shelter such as rocks or submerged logs. They will often nest next to other Sunfish species causing hybridization. The male aggressively defends his nest from other males using visual displays and aggressive physical force when necessary. The female will lay over 2,000 eggs and leave them for the male to guard. He keeps watch over the eggs until they hatch in three to five days, while protecting them and fanning them with his fins, keeping them clean, and providing them with oxygenated water. After the eggs hatch and the fry become free swimming, the male will court another female to lay eggs in the same nest.

Rainbow Darter

This small and very colorful fish is found in gravel and rubble riffles in small, fast-moving streams and small to medium-sized rivers. It grows to only 2 to 3 inches in length.

Dustin Lynch, Arkansas Natural Heritage Commission

A good indicator of water quality, this species is very sensitive to pollution and silt, staying in clean, pollution-free water.

The stunningly handsome Rainbow Darter is easily identified by three dark spots on the back, and blue and orange on the dorsal and anal fins. It is a small Perch-like fish that can be found in the Kings River. Like most Darter species, the male is more colorful than the female especially during breeding season. Breeding occurs when water temperature is 62 *F in the spring. This varies by location but is usually around April and May. Males defend their nesting territory in shallow riffles. The blue coloration in males becomes more intense during the spawn. A female lays 3-7 eggs for each spawning act. The eggs are fertilized and fall in the gravel with no parental care. This may be repeated many times over several days during the breeding season. A female can lay 800-1000 eggs each season. The eggs hatch in 10 to 11.5 days. Rainbow Darters will eat small crustaceans, snails and insects. Most gamefish of the Kings River are predators to the rainbow darter.

Largemouth Bass

The Largemouth Bass can be found in all areas of the Kings River but mainly makes its home in larger numbers on what is considered the lower Kings River below the J.D. Fletcher Public Access point. Here the river gradient and substrate produce an ideal habitat with deeper and slower moving pools, as the Kings finishes cutting its 90 mile journey through the mountains to Table Rock Lake.

This beautiful lake is known as one of the best fishing lakes in the Ozarks for Largemouth Bass as well as other game fish. The Largemouth Bass has a lot of the same char-  acteristics of the Spotted Bass including a very slender elongated body and coloration. What sets this fish far apart from the Smallmouth Bass or the Spotted Bass is its large mouth with the upper jaw line extending past the eye.

These bass have a dark band of irregular spots which do not form continuous rows. A deep notch almost completely separates the dorsal and spinal fins. The back and the sides of this fish are olive to green in color. These fish are most often found near logs or large rocks in deeper, slower-moving water. They primarily feed on other fish, crayfish, frogs, and insects. They have also been known to eat small birds and mice.

Spawning occurs in Arkansas from April to June when waters reach around 62*F. Circular depressions are made for nests on gravel bottoms where there is little current. The male will guard the nest until the fry becomes free-swimming. These fish can easily grow to 20" or more.

Walleye

The Walleye, sometimes called the yellow pike, can also be found on the Kings River. They are mainly olive and gold in color. The dorsal side is olive with some golden hues broken up by five darker saddles extending to the upper sides. The color shades to white on the belly. It has a very large mouth armed with very sharp teeth. They have large eyes with excellent eyesight and can see under low illumination levels. They tend to feed at dawn and dusk on cloudy overcast days

and under choppy water conditions when light penetration is disrupted. Walleye can grow up to 20 pounds with lengths as long as 31 inches. The Walleye of the Kings River live mainly in Table Rock Lake but migrate upriver in the early spring or late winter to spawn. Walleye travel in schools in spring and fall.

Spawning occurs when water temperatures reach 43-50*F, and usually in shallow water. A female can lay 500,000 eggs and no care is given by the male or female parent to the eggs or fry. Walleye feed mainly on crayfish and minnows.

MAMMALS OF THE KINGS RIVER

The Kings River is teeming with wildlife. It would not be uncommon to see mammals such as white-tailed deer, raccoon, mink, muskrat, beaver, feral hogs, or river otter, looking for food along a gravel bar or scurrying along the bank that they call home.

BIRDS OF THE KINGS RIVER

Arkansas is home to over 380 different types of birds. Some of these birds migrate to the Kings River seasonally. One of the most common birds you will see on the Kings River is the Great Blue Heron.

This large bird stands almost 4 feet tall and can be found fishing along any stretch of the Kings River. Several Native American tribes look at the Great Blue Heron as a sign of patience and good luck. It was believed, if you spotted a Heron, it meant good luck will be with you for a successful fishing trip.

Green Herons can also be seen along the banks of the Kings. This brown and green bird is a very small version of the Heron family. At only about 18" in length, the Green Heron is one of the few types of birds that uses tools. It will sometimes drop bait onto the surface of the water to attract small fish drawn to the bait. Like fishermen, this crafty bird has been known to use a variety of baits and lures, including insects, worms, twigs, and feathers to entice its next meal.

The Belted Kingfisher can also be seen flying low along the river looking for fish. This bird is uniquely built with a sturdy body, short tail, and large head and bill. The top of its body is blue and the underneath is white with a blue band across the chest. These birds run up and down the river and shorelines rattling their loud and unique call while looking and diving toward their aquatic prey such as small fish, crayfish, insects, small snakes, and even small mammals.

The migrating Bald Eagle calls the Kings River its home during the fall and winter months. Some of these birds now stay year around. This large bird with its white head and white tail is easily identifiable. Its primary food source is fish, and the Kings River provides what these birds crave. Once endangered, this majestic bird and national symbol has made an amazing comeback and can be seen nesting along the bluff lines or in the top of large trees along any stretch of the Kings River.

Other birds that can be seen along the Kings River include the Kildeer, Turkey Vulture, Cliff Swallow, Louisiana Waterthrush, and Wild Turkey. For more detailed information on these birds visit www.BirdsofArkansas.org.

SNAKES OF THE KINGS RIVER

There are many species of snakes in Arkansas. Thirty-six are non-venomous with six being venomous. The most common snake seen on the Kings River is the Midland Water Snake. This snake is often mistaken for a Copperhead with colors and patterns being somewhat similar. Unlike the head of a Copperhead, the head of a Midland Water Snake is narrow, and the eyes are round. Copperheads truly have the appearance of the copper color, whereas the water snake has more of a light brown color. It is very rare to see a Copperhead in the water unless it is swimming on top of the water to get to another side of the bank. Midland Water Snakes are fast and excellent swimmers on top and underneath the water.

The Cottonmouth is probably the most common venomous snake you will see on the Kings River. This species of pit viper is also called a Water Moccasin. They have large, triangular heads with a dark line through the eye and elliptical pupils. They are a heavy-bodied snake and can vary in color. They can be completely dark in color (brown or black) or have dark crossbands and a brown and yellow color. As pit vipers they have large triangular heads. These snakes can be seen during the day but forage primarily after dark eating crayfish, frogs, fish, and small mammals. The Cottonmouth receives its name from the whiteness of the interior of the mouth it exposes during a defensive display. Leave these and all snakes alone and they will leave you alone.

Kings River Legend Bud Stoppel

Another local legend that could be seen floating down stretches of the Kings River in a wooden, flat-bottomed boat is Bud Stoppel. Bud grew up fairly poor and fishing the bountiful Kings River helped keep the Stoppel family fed during hard times. Bud had to learn fishing skills at an early age to take care of his big family. An Indian chief taught Bud's father how to fish, and the Stoppel family has passed it down several generations. Bud was a natural at fishing and was known to use mostly live bait to catch all fish of the Kings River. He also teamed up with legend J.D. Fletcher to help guide many fishermen who were attracted to the great fishing found on the Kings River.

Keith Pendergraft describes fishing the Kings River with Bud back in the late 60's.

It was 1968 or '69, I can't be sure but I had been to my grandmother's house in Eureka for Christmas about six months before. My father Floyd and I along with the rest of the family, were headed back to Eureka Springs for two weeks in late May. My father had promised me a surprise fishing trip on the Kings River with one of his old schoolmates from Eureka Springs. We had always done a lot of swimming in the Kings where it went under Hwy 62 Bridge. Usually, while the family was swimming, I would wade up the river and fish where the Osage and Kings met. I was fascinated by the Smallmouth Bass and the clear cool water. I had read several articles in either Field and Stream, Sports Afield, or Outdoor Life, about the Smallmouth Bass

in the Kings River and the men who guided fishermen in quest for a trophy Smallmouth.

Two days later my father told me we were going fishing in the morning with one of his old friends who was a guide on the Kings River. His name was Bud Stoppel, a man my father said knew the Kings well. That night I was excited as a kid on Christmas Eve and gathered my fishing gear together along with my two poles. I barely slept a wink.

The next morning we waited for Bud on the side of Hwy 62 by what is now Myrtie-Mae's, right across from the Joy Motel in Eureka Springs. It was not long before a truck with a flat-bottomed boat pulled up alongside us. Out stepped a man who had a big smile on his face shaking my father's hand and then mine. His face and arms were well tanned from the sun and he was wearing a dark red baseball cap with a tiger on it. After all the formalities, we drove to a town called Grandview just off Hwy 62. I asked my father if it was all right if I rode with Bud, and he said it was fine if Bud didn't mind. I talked to Bud all the way to the river about the baits I needed to have tied on my fishing pole, the water conditions we would encounter, and how many types of bass they had in the Kings River. It seemed like forever but we finally arrived at the place where we were going to launch his flat-bottom boat. The bank was rather steep but we managed to get the boat in the river with no problems along with all the gear.

I stayed with the boat while Bud and my father shuttled their trucks to a place named Stoney Point. I organized all the gear in the boat while waiting for their return. We loaded up in the old flat-bottom boat, which had seen its share of dents and scratches but was still sound. Bud sat in the back and I sat in the middle seat with my father in the front.

As we began drifting down the river, Bud said this was the 5th or 6th time he had floated this stretch of river this year. The entire time we fished Bud was talking about the river. He talked about how someone else or himself caught a fish by this big rock, tree limb, eddy or gravel bar. I cast for about 20 minutes without a strike. Bud had already caught five little Smallmouths and I was getting discouraged. I think Bud sensed this. He tapped my shoulder, handed me a pat, and said, "you may want to try this." I think it was a Bill Norman or Rebel crank bait which was crawfish colored. As I tied it on Bud said, "cast that bait behind that rock where the water is still." It didn't take a half dozen turns of the reel handle and I had a good strike. I was overly excited and Bud told me to calm down and play the fish. Bud netted the "brownie" and I took him out of the net. My first nice Kings River Smallmouth which Bud said weighed around 2 1/2 pounds. Little did I know this was just the first of many Smallmouth I would catch that day. It wasn't five minutes later I had another  one in the boat. Bud said, "You are catching on now." My father chimed in and said, "Bud, my son wasn't raised around here like me and you, so he might seem a little slow at first." Both of them had a big grins on their faces after that comment, which made me more comfortable being around two great fisherman.

I watched Bud effortlessly paddle the boat down the river while still having a chance to make a lot of casts and give me Tips on where to cast next. It was amazing to me he could keep the boat moving along easily and still do other things. Little did I know at the time this was a good lesson on becoming a river fisherman.

It was almost mid-morning and my arm was already showing signs of overuse. Bud said, "Do you hear that bullfrog up ahead." I nodded my head, letting him know I did. He said, "If I can spot him sitting on the bank, I will catch him on this bait." He shook the old yellowed fiberglass rod with a red and white

Baby Lucky 13 on it. I thought this was some type of old hillbilly joke sort of like snipe hunting at night back home. My father was grinning ear-to-ear. Bud was scanning the bank looking for the frog. Bud and my father were smiling again, which was a sign the joke would be on me. Bud hollered, "There he is," and cast the bait toward the bank. It wasn't until the frog moved that I saw him. The bait had landed within six inches of him, and the frog awkwardly covered the distance quickly and did a nosedive on the Lucky 13. Bud set the hook and the frog had all he could handle. It was unlike any fight I had ever seen on a rod and reel. He got it to the boat and got him unhooked and put it in a small ice chest with our lunch. He said, "Your Grandma can fix him up real good tonight with the fish, taters, and pie." I was shocked at what I had just witnessed, and it would be years before I pulled off the feat myself on Lake Leatherwood outside of Eureka Springs.

The sun was up high and my stomach was growling. Bud and my father must have had the same feeling, as we paddled toward a nice shady gravel bar. We all got out and passed around the Ritz crackers, red rind cheese, and a few 'pops' as Bud called them. Bud talked about all the fish we had caught and how we would catch even more as the sun started down. He looked in my tackle box and suggested a few of the baits I had in there for later. Bud pointed out a few fish on the stringer. He said, "I know you can tell which of these are smallmouths but can you tell the difference between a Largemouth Bass and a Kentucky Bass?" I thought for a second and said, "I don't really know." Bud said, "Feel the tongue on the bass and then this one." I did as he asked. He said, "Did you notice that one had a real rough tongue and the other was real slick? The rough-tongued bass was a Kentucky Bass. This is the easiest and surest way to tell."

After that lesson, Bud said we still had about four hours left, so we'd better get moving. As we started down the river I asked Bud about the bream in the river. He said we have all *types of bream or sunfish in the Kings.* "Put that little catalpa-colored beetle spin on." *First cast I caught a nice goggle eye. After that it seemed I was catching a fish almost every cast. I had completely forgotten I was tired. My father and Bud quit fishing for a while after lunch and resorted to talking about the old times. I continued to fish as Bud would suggest places to cast while conversing with my father.*

We only had a couple hours to fish as Bud and the river glided the boat toward our destination. We started throwing a variety of top water baits. One of the baits Bud was casting made a lot of noise on the water. The bait had something like a spinner or propeller on it and the bass loved it. Years later, this bait would be called a lunker lure or a buzz bait. They would strike the bait with a vengeance. The Hula Popper, Jitterbug, and the Rapala, were poison to the bass. The old Devils Horse caught its share as well. We landed some smallmouths over four pounds that afternoon with some largemouths in the middle-to-upper five pound range.

It was getting late, and I was getting worried we would still be floating in the dark. I made the mistake of asking Bud if he had a flashlight. My father and Bud had a good laugh about that. Bud commented we would be at the takeout landing in less than 30 minutes. I sort of relaxed after hearing this, and I asked, "Bud, do you ever get tired of paddling all day?" He said, "No, I just know how to read the river and let it take me where I want to go." I was surprised how little effort he had used to maneuver the boat with a slight touch of the paddle in the river. It would be several more fishing trips with him before I began to comprehend what he was actually telling me.

We finally made it to Stoney Point, and I was exhausted. We loaded the boat and gear up in Bud's truck and headed toward where we put in, to get the other truck. I fell asleep on the highway driving back to Eureka that night. It all seemed like a *dream but the next morning I realized it wasn't when I had to clean all the fish and one big bullfrog.*

That was over 50 years ago now but the memories of that trip and others on the Kings with Bud and my father make it seem like yesterday. They have both long since passed on but the knowledge I gained in those eitght or ten trips has grown with time and will always be with me. I have passed what I learned to my son who has a great love for fishing, especially for the brown bass we call the Smallmouth. I hope the tradition continues forever on the Kings River.
~ Keith Pendergraft

Gage Lugo, great nephew of Bud Stoppel

VI. ABOUT THE AUTHOR (Doug "Riverman" Allen)

The 5 stages of fishing:

Stage 1 - I just want to catch fish.
Stage 2 - I want to catch a lot of fish.
Stage 3 - I want to catch big fish.
Stage 4 - I'm just happy to be fishing.
Stage 5 - I want to pass on my knowledge and passion about fishing.

At this age in my life, I'm happily in stage 5. I entered this stage a few years ago teaching my kids to fish the Kings River. I bet you can see different stages in the things you love. Running? Gardening? Biking? Playing music? Painting? I love to teach others and get immense pleasure when the enlightenment comes and they understand that it's not really about the fish anymore. I have a favorite fish (Smallmouth Bass) but as I've gotten older I realized it's never been about the fish. It's the experience. I'm gonna write it down and pass it on. I fondly remember and appreciate those that passed it on to me.

BACKGROUND

Born and raised in the hills of Northwest Arkansas, my home on Onyx Cave Road was just a couple of dirt miles away from the Kings River. We lived just outside the quaint little tourist town of Eureka Springs. Arkansas fisherman and biologists form my family tree, and planted seeds of passion for anything related to bodies of water. After a lifetime of fishing everything from creeks, farm ponds, lakes, and especially rivers, my love of water is now deep and wide. Swimming, canoeing, and fishing most stretches of the Kings River, filled my summer days. The twists and turns of the river are as familiar to me as the back of my hand. Now I live in Fayetteville, Arkansas, which allows me to sneak away to kayak, guide, or wade fish, nearly year around.

My mother was the best barehanded crawdad catcher I have ever seen, and my dad was a fine Smallmouth Bass fisherman and teacher. From them I learned appreciation for the Arkansas waterways, especially the Kings River, like some people are taught the family business. The angling disciplines were taught and applied to life as naturally as the sun rises and sets. My Irish transplanted wife, Pauline and I are raising our own crew of river rats, including two daughters and a son.

As a guide and steward of the river, I teach others to kayak and fish while leaving them with a piece of information or appreciation for the surroundings. It all aligns when I do my job well. If they listen closely and observe the patterns of the river, perhaps they might just catch a few fish in the process.

"The river calls to each of us. I feel its pulse, I long for it when I'm away. It is a part of who I am."
~ The Riverman

RIVERMAN MEMORIES

"Give a man a fish and he will eat for a day, Teach him to fish on the Kings River and you will have memories for a lifetime."
~ Riverman

Drowning

My earliest memory of the Kings River came as a young child about the age of four, near Keels Creek on the Kings River. One summer day, my father (the original Riverman) took my whole family to the Kings River for an afternoon of fishing and swimming. My dad was mostly fishing. He was dressed in cutoff jeans, army boots without socks, no shirt, and binoculars around his neck to bird watch. He was carrying his pride and joy which was a Mitchel Garcia rod and reel in one hand strung with a 6-pound test line, a gold number 2 size hook and a metal crawdad bucket full of live bait in the other. I thought he was the coolest thing ever. My Dad!! He was an avid Smallmouth Bass fisherman and came from a family of biologist/naturalists. He and the world's greatest crawdad catcher, my mom, had just caught a bucket of live crawdads for that day's fishing adventure. Dad decided to take the bucket of crawdads downstream to do a little Smallmouth Bass fishing. He began to make his way down the river and little did he know that his four-year-old son was following the Riverman. His long strides soon left me behind but that was no matter. I was going to catch up with this mighty fisherman carrying the neatest fishing gear, and a bucket full of live crawdads I was dying to play with, naming each one. I slowly made my way downstream after him without "Rivermom" being aware. Suddenly, I stepped into a deep pool and found myself sinking to the gravel at the bottom. I re-

member, like it was yesterday, the ripples of the crystal clear cool water going by and the small silver flashing minnows swimming back and forth in front of my face as my eyes were wide open in wonderment. It happened so quickly I wasn't quite sure what was happening, but after the initial shock of the cold water, I was calm. What felt like forever was probably only less than a minute and then everything began to get dark. I was drowning. Then it went black. I wasn't scared. I felt at peace. The next memory I had was sitting on the hood of my Dad's 1970 green Chevy stepside pickup as he was patting me on the back telling me to cough. "You're going to be okay, son." I could see my mom next to him and hear her panicked voice pick out a couple of choice words for my father as the water was clearing from every orifice in my head. Since that day, I've had a special connection to the Kings River, and experience being at home when I'm there. I feel its pulse, so to speak. I long for it when I'm away. Drawn to the water like a dowsing rod. My dad always reminded me I caused him to ruin his expensive binoculars. My mom always reminded my dad he almost caused her only son to drown. I was very lucky that day in more ways than one. Over the years, my family and friends have had many great days on the Kings River. Shooting the rapids in a kayak or catching crawdads, hellgrammites, minnows and Smallmouth Bass. I love teaching each one the special intricacies of this extraordinary water resource. It's important to note not one of my "riverkids" have drowned following me down the river. I told my wife when I die, my wishes are for her to cremate my body and sprinkle my ashes across the river at my favorite fishing hole below a big bluff near where I came close to drowning many moons ago. She has promised to do that, so the Smallmouth Bass would eat me and get a little payback. Turnabout is fair play.

Dirt Road

I left the concrete world today. Took a right turn. Something pulled me in that direction. Some would call it old Berryville Road just outside of Eureka Springs. I took a drive back in time. Down what was once a dirt road full of kids in backs of pickup trucks, legs dangling off, watermelon in the cooler, crawdad bucket and fishing poles clanking off the bed of the truck. Mouthfuls of dust and eyes matted from the county dirt road. Dads long arm hanging out of the old Chevy truck window and resting on the door mirror. I could see the reflection of his face in the mirror with his dark tinted glasses, and sharp chin. I drove past one of the most spectacular sights you could possibly view of the river valley and mountains, toward Berryville. Made my way past what I always called the Brashear Berry Farm where we picked strawberries one summer for Lynn Brashear. 25 cents for every pint we picked, and all you can eat while picking them! My back never hurt so bad, and all I could think about was the river nearby. Or I would fantasize about catching big catfish in the deep, green, mossy-covered Brashear pond. Just below the "berry farm" I drove across a low water spring and made my way to Keels Creek where as a child we caught buckets of crawdads for bait to catch the mighty Smallmouth Bass. Occasionally, we would hang the crawdads off our ears and call them Ozark earrings. I'm not sure what was more fun, catching crawdads or catching fish. We would eventually make our way down the gravel creek bed of Keels Creek where it met the free-flowing Kings River.

Harrison Sutcliffe Photography

A huge swimming hole formed at the confluence, and at times a risky and usually frayed rope swing dared us to swing across a root ball from a fallen tree. That root ball was one of the best fishing holes on the river!!! "Don't swim it until we fish it. You'll spook the fish!" Dad, the fisherman, always said as we approached the local favorite swimming hole. I also remember a few Water Moccasins hanging out in that ideal snake habitat, and they were probably the reason my mom never did swim in it with us. I remember my dad always walking ahead of us to make sure there weren't any skinny dippers or "hippies" as he called them, in the swimming hole to scar our virgin eyes. Mom, the family expert crawdad catcher, always lagged behind and met us later with a noisy metal bucket full of crawdads the perfect size to entice a strike from the king of the Kings, the Smallmouth Bass.

Today, to my surprise, there was a sign on the remnants of the old concrete bridge threatening prosecution if trespassed upon. What? Didn't they know this was sacred ground? How can this be? A bridge that connected us with fun adventures, and storytelling for years to come. Although the swimming hole is no longer there and only remnants of concrete pillars remain of the bridge, it will always be intact and tucked away safely in my memories to cross whenever I want.

A Hot Spring County Memory

"Although this article is not about the Kings River, it holds a special place in my heart as it was written eloquently by my talented Aunt Pat Wilson about her brother that died from brain cancer. My Uncle Kenneth Allen was an amazing marine biologist and I'll never forget floating the Kings River with him and my dad. My Uncle Kenneth irritating my dad, the serious fisherman, by snorkeling alongside the flat-bottom boat, identifying and spooking all the fish he could see before my dad was able to cast. I was lucky to be among greatness that day and find myself fortunate to be educated about fish and habitat by two of the finest Smallmouth fishermen and biologists in Arkansas. They both left this world too soon but their influence lives on."

Dear Editor,

I'm usually not an early riser but this particular morning while visiting my brother Ken in Malvern, I found him having breakfast at 6 am. He was always an early riser, since the time we were children at Bismarck, and he had to get up at 4:30 every morning to milk cows before leaving for school. Ken asked me to go riding with him, and we drove to the nearby historic Rockport Bridge which spanned the Ouachita River.

The wooden bridge had recently been closed to traffic because it was in danger of collapsing. Ken pointed out the bridge was actually leaning upstream, against the rushing waters, which were undermining its foundation.

We spent the rest of that beautiful morning exploring the rocky river bank and sharing our mutual interest in and appreci-

ation for the beauty of the state we grew up in, left, then returned to over and over again because it was home and because we loved it.

That day, we came across some fishermen who weren't having much luck, and my brother explained the best angling techniques.

They looked at the emaciated man with wide surgical scars across the top of his head—bald from chemotherapy for brain cancer—and little did they know they were getting advice from an expert. A man with a doctorate in marine biology, and who had taught residents of Saudi Arabia how to raise catfish—in spite of the fact the country has no fresh water streams.

In eight months, at age 54, the cancer claimed Ken, and the Rockport Bridge was swept away by a flood in less than a year. But both still exist in my collection of precious memories.

- Pat Allen Wilson

Sneaky Kings River Snake

It was late morning on the day of the solar eclipse, August 21st, 2017. I was excited to break away from work and spend an afternoon on the beautiful Kings River and fish for Smallmouth Bass while experiencing this rare and intriguing event. Joining me was dog trainer and dog whisperer, Denise Holmes, from the popular blog Travel Tales and her obedient dog Henri.

They took me up on my open invitation to take them on their maiden voyage in a kayak down the beautiful Kings River to witness this rare and extraordinary event. The solar eclipse I observed on the Kings River was absolutely magnificent but that's another fish-catching story for another time. This is about a snake. A sneaky snake.

As we arrived at the access area at Ernie's, Kings River Outfitters, I gave her a little speech about what to expect on the river and very subtly mentioned that we might spot a snake or two and that most of them were nonvenomous and mostly stayed on the bank. You leave them alone, they leave you alone. I saw a raised eyebrow and a nod of the head acknowledging that today's adventure might include spotting different critters along the mighty Kings. We loaded our gear and took off down the river for a great experience on the water!

I usually assume that most folks can steer a kayak pretty well. I assumed wrong with kayak beginner Denise. Bless her heart. For the first 1/4 mile she managed to cover a lot of water going bank to bank and getting turned backwards in the eddies.

Fortunately for me, the river flows north and eventually pushes everything down river including Denise and her dog Henri so I knew we would eventually get to our destination. As a trained Riverman, most of my friends and family know that my head is always on a swivel looking for unusual movements in the water or bank that usually mean some kind of snake, turtle, fish or other river wildlife. I usually identify snakes fairly quickly and will even catch them to educate the people about one of nature's creatures. As I made my way ahead of Denise through  our first set of rapids, I spotted a snake curled up on the bank. As I got closer, I identified it as a cottonmouth. 99% of the snakes I see on the Kings are nonvenomous and misidentified by most people. Unfortunately, these Midland Water Snakes are unnecessarily killed. But what are the odds we would be 15 minutes into our float and see a venomous snake? I said nothing as I went on by, thinking it was far enough away and posed no threat as we were not disturbing it. I wasn't going to say a word about it. Best not to alarm the river rookie since I didn't know how Denise and her dog Henri, would react. As my new kayak friend was zig-zagging anything but straight through the wide run, I noticed the snake had entered the water. It was a pretty good size snake and was deliberately making a top water swim to the opposite bank completely unaware of two kayakers coincidentally passing through its habitat at the same time. Probably could care less. To my amazement, this cottonmouth had chosen an angle that would intercept Denise, Henri, and her zig-zagging kayak, about half way down the rapids. I remember thinking to myself. "No way this is happening. Geez, I'm gonna have to paddle upstream as fast as I can and grab that snake once it slithers into her kayak. Is the dog gonna freak out? Can he swim?" I turned around and was paddling up stream

but could not get there quickly enough, due to the strength of the current. Maybe Denise wouldn't spot the snake. No harm, no foul, right? Nope. "Um, Doug, there is a snake heading right for me. What do I do?" I thought of many scenarios but only could muster up a few words of encouragement. "Paddle backwards and it will just swim on by." I was taking a line out of an old movie called Top Gun when the pilot put on the brakes of the plane as they were being chased, and the enemy plane flew right by. I laughed out loud. What was I thinking? She could barely paddle forward let alone backwards. Luckily, Denise and her zig-zagging kayaking skills came in handy. Just as the snake reached the kayak, she paddled the wrong side moving the keel just enough to allow the snake to swim on by without a bother. Crisis avoided! Smooth sailing from here! The rest of the trip was uneventful as far as snakes were concerned. She never mentioned the snake and apparently it didn't rattle her too bad. Henri and Denise were great sports, and I'll never forget that sneaky snake on the river along with Denise and Henri's excellent kayaking skills.

The Fish Stalker

I was 8 years old at the time. So this would make it around middle May, 1978, in Carroll County. Dad would never fish the mighty Kings before May. "You're wasting your time son. Water is up in April and not the right temperature. Crawdads aren't out of hibernation yet. Be patient." He didn't need a water gauge. He knew the depth, color and right temperature when the river was ready.

He knew by experience. May was his favorite month to fish. In the 70's, there was very little "fishing pressure" on the Kings River and the old creaky plank suspension bridge on old Berryville Road was still operable and traveled by mainly locals daring enough to keep both wheels on the randomly nailed and warped planks. I anxiously awaited my dad to get home from work. My dad, a hard-working microbiologist by trade and a passionate fisherman by heart, worked long hours at St. Mary's Hospital in Rogers with an hour drive home to Eureka Springs. He didn't arrive at our home on Onyx Cave Road until 5:30-6 pm. How excited I was to see him! It was always an adventure with the Riverman! He quickly changed into cut off jeans, army boots and wore an old sleeveless hooded sweatshirt no matter what the temperature was outside. It only took a few minutes to drive the old 1970 short-bed green stepside Chevy down to the timeless old bridge of the Kings that was only a couple of miles from our house. A house of fishermen and fisherwomen. A house of crawdad catchers. It would be dark in an hour or so. Upon arrival and gathering our fishing poles with six-pound test line, #2 gold hook, and a metal crawdad (minnow) bucket we would carefully climb our way off the side of the old bridge down steep steps made naturally by the overhanging rocks and traveled smooth by fisherman and many local swimmers. A quick jump over the last few weeds and into the clear, cool water of the Kings.

First order of business was to catch bait. Crawdads were on the fish menu tonight and my dad would turn over only the bigger flat rocks to find a crawdad the size that he liked to use. That day he chose an oversized 6" crawdad versus his usual 2" crawdad. I noticed he was being picky and only capturing a few of the larger green colored long pincered crawdads native to the Kings River. With a fair amount of crawfish and gear in hand, we slowly waded our way downstream to a particular hole in the river that my dad told me held a couple of really big Smallmouth Bass. We didn't have much time before it got dark, and getting caught on the river after dark is not a fun experience but my dad didn't seem concerned. I wasn't concerned either. I was with the Riverman.

During our walk, my dad told me about what excellent eyesight and hearing Smallmouth Bass had. They can see you coming from many feet away. They can also hear the crunch of the gravel under your feet. You have to sneak up on the big ones. We stopped about 20 yards short of our destination, and dad motioned me to get down on my belly. My dad, the seasoned army vet, and myself, crawled on our bellies across the gravel bank within 15 feet of the fishing hole of his choice. He pointed at two very large fish directly in the middle of his "honey hole." Quietly he said, "Son, we are going after big bass today." He carefully picked out two lively and large long pincered green crawdads out of the bucket being careful not to close the metal lid loudly, which would spook the fish. He instructed me to wait with my crawdad until he had a fish on, explaining to me that often when you catch a Smallmouth Bass, another will follow and try to steal the bait out of the first one's mouth as it's frantically trying to get away. I was to stand up and immediately throw my crawdad after my dad had his fish on.

My dad baited his hook carefully through the backside of the crawdad tail and while still laying down, cocked his body to the side, clicked open his bail to his classic Mitchel Garcia reel as if pulling a pin out of a grenade and brilliantly lobbed his live ammunition of choice within a couple of feet of those two enormous fish targets. Within seconds one of the bass sucked in the lively and active oversized crawdad that had hit the water running like a scolded dog. He waited, making sure the crawdad was completely in the mouth of the fish and watched as the six pound test line was leaving the spool as he purposely left the bail open. Suddenly without warning he yelled "Now," jumped up, and in one motion he closed the bail to his reel and set the hook violently. Fish on! What a fight and dad was right another bass was following it trying to steal the bait out of its mouth. I threw my crawdad at this aggressive fish and sure enough, I had a fish on too! Not as big as the one my dad hooked but big enough for this youngster to wrestle. We both fought our fish with the sound of the drag of our reels screaming as we landed our fish at the same time. Both of us with smiles and dad nodding his head in approval.

My dad had a rare four pound Smallmouth Bass, and I had a two pound Smallmouth Bass. At that time we took both fish home to eat. It was not uncommon for us to have fish many nights of the week with a batch of fried potatoes. However, I am now strictly catch-and-release and have not eaten a Smallmouth Bass since I was a kid.

As we were walking back upstream towards the bridge, fish dragging behind us on a stringer, I asked my dad how he knew those two bass were there? He stopped, put his hand on my shoulder and said, "Sometimes I fish alone, son; and I saw these bass one day and wanted you to experience and learn something amazing." I was a little hurt to know that my dad had gone fishing without me. But as I've gotten older and experienced many stressful life events, I understand that this was his peace and his get away. His river. His time. Now it's my river. Thanks Dad. I understand. I'll pass it on.

Duane Hada (Ozark Bass)

Catching Crawdads

I can remember catching crawdads with my mom and dad near Keels Creek on the Kings River. My dad was always on the lookout for snakes. He would see one and know it was there. He wouldn't say anything to my mom or us kids. But after he identified the snake as nonvenomous, he would quickly reach out and snatch it by the neck and hold it out toward my mom just to see her reaction. One day after my dad boldly caught another snake and presented it toward her like a bouquet of flowers, she threw the whole damn bucket of crawdads at him. An hour's worth of work and now no fish bait. He never did that to her again

Passing It On

I was at the Kings River below the Hwy 62 Bridge yesterday and shared the gravel bank with Juanita Drought Crider and her young students doing water quality studies for Clear Spring School. I noticed a little girl following me around, and she even waded out into the cold water to ask me what I was doing. She quizzed me on my fishing pole and the fact I had waterproof waders on while her boots were filling up with very cold water still not very warm from the cold winter we had. I asked her if she had ever fished before. She said no but she remembered her father did before he died. Kinda shocked me when she said that. So young. So I asked her if she would like to cast a line with my fishing pole. Her face lit up as she became very excited. We had to quickly review the terms reel, line, bail and rod in order for her to understand how to throw it. After a few practice casts she got the hang of it and was thrilled even though she didn't catch anything. Her feet were cold and she moved on back to the group to finish their water studies.

I caught a decent sized fish about 30 minutes later. She must have been watching, because she raced over to see it. We looked at the fish and I explained the species with the different traits about the type of bass it was. A smallmouth. I asked her if she wanted to hold it. Her eyes got big and she simply nodded. She said nothing. I showed her how to pinch her thumb and forefinger together in order to hold the fish gently from the lower mouth. After a moment she got the courage to hold the fish. She held it and squealed with excitement. Before I could say or teach her how to let it go, she turned and raced up the bank toward her class, carrying the fish the way I had showed her. I thought to myself, "Oh no! There goes that poor fish." I waited a minute while pictures were taken and then nicely yelled across the riverbank it was time to let it go, please. Juanita must have heard me and agreed, and the little girl kinda flung the poor fish back into the shallow edge of the water without using much of a gentle catch-and-release method. Of course not, it was the first fish she had ever held. I just kinda waved at her in approval but watched intently as the fish made its way to deeper water apparently as fine as can be.

I hope the little girl keeps that day in her memory. Maybe a new fisherman was born. Take a kid fishing would ya.

We all live downstream...

"Once I leave the river behind and I return to my concrete world, all the water drains out through my toes and is replaced by thoughts of paying mortgages, making payroll and raising kids. My soul is back there."

~ Doug Allen, October 2018

BRIDGES OF THE KINGS RIVER

Riverman's Guide 103

Information Resources:

Kings River Website
www.KingsRiverArkansas.com

Arkansas Game and Fish Commission
2 Natural Resources Drive
Little Rock, AR 72205
www.AGFC.com
800-364-4263

U.S. Army Corps of Engineers
Little Rock District
P.O. Box 867
Little Rock, AR 72203
www.swl.usace.army.mil
501-324-5551

Kings River Watershed Partnership
P.O. Box 961
Berryville, AR 72616
870-480-8897
www.kingsriverwatershed.org

Arkansas Department of Environmental Quality
5301 Northshore Dr.
North Little Rock, AR 72118-5317
501-682-0744
www.adeq.state.ar.us

Arkansas Department of Parks And Tourism
One Capital Mall
Little Rock, AR 72201
www.arkansas.com
501-682-7777

Arkansas Forestry Commission
1 Natural Resources Dr
Little Rock, AR 72205
www.forestry.arkansas.gov
501-225-1598

The Nature Conservancy of Arkansas
601 North University Avenue
Little Rock, AR 72205
www.nature.org
501-663-6699

Ozark National Forest
605 West Main
Russellville, AR 72801
www.stateparks.com
479-964-7200

Arkansas Natural Resources Commission
101 East Capitol, Suite 350
Little Rock, AR 72201
www.anrc.arkansas.gov
501-682-1611

Stream Team Program
Arkansas Game and Fish Commission
2 Natural Resource Drive
Little Rock, AR 72205
501-223- 6428

Made in the USA
Middletown, DE
18 January 2022

59063156R00060